Business Civilization

in Decline

Books by Robert L. Heilbroner
Business Civilization in Decline
An Inquiry into the Human Prospect
Between Capitalism and Socialism
The Economic Problem
The Limits of American Capitalism
A Primer on Government Spending
(with Peter L. Bernstein)
The Great Ascent
The Making of Economic Society
The Future as History
The Quest for Wealth
The Worldly Philosophers

Robert L. Heilbroner

Business Civilization
in Decline

W · W · NORTON & COMPANY, INC ·

NEW YORK

FIRST EDITION

Library of Congress Cataloging in Publication Data
Heilbroner, Robert L
  Business civilization in decline.
  Includes bibliographical references.
  1. Capitalism. 2. Industry—Social aspects. 3. Civilization,
Modern—1950– 4. Economic forecasting. I. Title.
HB501.H397   330.9′04   75–33367
ISBN 0–393–05571–X
ISBN 0–393–09184–8 pbk.

Published simultaneously in Canada
by George J. McLeod Limited, Toronto

PRINTED IN THE UNITED STATES OF AMERICA

1   2   3   4   5   6   7   8   9

Acknowledgments

The essays referred to in the Preface include the following:

Chapter I relates in part to "Phase Two of the Capitalist System," *The New York Times Magazine,* November 28, 1971.

Chapter II draws on "Has Capitalism a Future?" prepared for a conference sponsored by Industriegewerkshaft Metall in Oberhausen, West Germany, on April 14, 1972. A somewhat shorter version appeared in *World,* September 12, 1972, entitled "The Future of Capitalism."

Chapter III was originally prepared for a conference under the auspices of the Japan Society and the Johnson Foundation. Parts of the essay appeared in somewhat different form in *Dissent* as "Economic Problems of a 'Postindustrial' Society," Spring 1973, and in *Prologue to the Future,* James Morley, ed. (Lexington, Mass.: D.C. Heath, 1973).

Chapter IV utilizes sections of two review essays that appeared in the *New York Review of Books,* February 11, 1971, and March 20, 1975.

Chapter V and the Preface incorporate portions of an introduction written for *Corporate Social Policy,* Robert Heilbroner and Paul London, eds. (Reading, Mass.: Addison-Wesley, 1975).

For Shirley

Contents

Preface

THESE CHAPTERS ARE explorations of a business civilization in decline. This does not imply that I think we are headed into a catastrophic depression or that inflation will ultimately prove to be a fatal disease. Both are possibilities, but I do not see them as the causes of the major challenges looming in the future. Even if a severe depression is avoided and inflation tamed or overcome, I still believe that the civilization of business—the civilization to which we give the name capitalism—is slated to disappear, probably not within our lifetimes but in all likelihood within that of our grandchildren and great grandchildren.

Some readers may find such a premise disconcerting because it smacks of radicalism. Hence perhaps I should begin by reminding them that there is nothing exclusively radical in the proposition that the business system is doomed. A huge literature, based on the work of Marx, has sought to demonstrate the impending demise of capitalism from its self-wrought malfunctions and "internal contradictions." But the anticipation of a coming end to the business order has not been confined to Marxian analysts. Joseph Schumpeter, a conservative theorist who admired the very institutions that Marx

9

detested, also concluded that the civilization built on business was incapable of long life. "Can capitalism survive?" he asked in *Capitalism, Socialism and Democracy*. He answered: "No. I do not think it can."

For Schumpeter, however, the villain in the piece was not an expected failure of the economic machinery: it was the underlying cast of mind characteristic of a business civilization—rational, calculating, skeptical. Such a mindset served capitalism well when its rise was opposed by the "irrational" privileges of an aristocratic order; but once in the saddle, Schumpeter maintained, this critical intellectuality would be turned against the pretensions of property and would reveal them to be as empty as those of nobility.

My own assessment draws on both Marxian and Schumpeterian insights, without following either slavishly. From the former it singles out prospective self-wrought changes in the milieu within which capitalist processes must work, and concludes that within our time frame these changes will pose problems of greater magnitude than we can plausibly expect the system to accommodate itself to. Meanwhile from the Schumpeterian critique it stresses challenges that undermine the culture rather than the system of business—challenges that weaken the spirit and values of what we call bourgeois society, thereby hastening its demise from within as well as from without.

But I do not want to anticipate the content of my chapters in this preface. Rather, I wish to take a few words to explain the genesis of this book. The great bulk of it derives from essays written over a period of years subsequent to the publication of *The Limits of American Capitalism* in 1965 and prior to the appearance of *An Inquiry into the Human Prospect* in 1974. I mention these books because there is a clear parallelism between many of the thoughts expressed in their pages and the ideas set forth here. Numerous ideas, even passages, can be traced to origins in the first book or to later expressions in the second.

It is this very parallelism that provides the rationale for the present book. For on rereading my essays, I was struck by the fact that they contained a theme that had not been fully developed in my preceding books—the theme of the "stages of change" through which a declining business civilization would have to pass. Accordingly, I decided to weld together the elements of this theme into a single argument, extending the perspective of my previous efforts to describe the trajectory of capitalism, and emphasizing aspects of the theme of capitalist decline that were only passed over hurriedly in my later book.

Someone who examines the citations in the Acknowledgments will, however, discover that I have not merely glued together the five essays mentioned there. Rather, the original essays have been used as source material to sustain and supplement my already expressed views from a somewhat different and more sharply focused perspective. Therefore I have added to, emended, and at times rearranged my earlier words to give unity to the problem I am addressing in these pages, without, I hope, doing violence to the intent of my original statements. If there is one tell-tale element testifying to the diverse origins of this book, it may lie in some variation of style from chapter to chapter, owing to the different audiences and occasions for which the earlier essays were written. I have decided to let that variation stand, to make clear the debt that the present book owes to my previous writings.

ONE

The Immediate Future

CAPITALISM IS drifting into planning. Is there anyone who would deny the fact? The problem is to interpret it, to place the drift in the perspective of a larger historic movement.

That is what I seek to do as an initial consideration of the larger theme of this book. For the problem raised by the drift into planning immediately provides an Ariadne's thread that will help us follow the argument to unfold in this and succeeding chapters. The argument concerns the tension between the economic machinery of capitalism—its business imperatives, its corporate bodies, its commercial relations—and the larger social order of capitalism, an order that embraces a political apparatus and a host of social institutions as well as an economic machinery. It will be my major thesis that the political apparatus within capitalism is steadily growing, enhancing its power, and usurping functions formerly delegated to the economic sphere—not to undo, but to preserve that sphere. In the end, I think this same political expansion will be a major factor in the extinction of the business civilization, but that takes me far beyond this initial chapter.

Let us begin, then, by considering the present. Everyone agrees that business has contracted its place within society over the last fifty years, crowded out by a growing government presence. Hence our first task is to gain some understanding of this basic shift. Does the enlargement of the political apparatus of the state in itself mean that business civilization is declining? Need we go no further than a recognition of this change to concede that capitalism is disappearing?

This central problem has been discussed many times. I would like to bring some freshness to the issue by considering the matter in an impressionistic, but I think not unrealistic way, from the points of view of two New Yorkers, both conveniently named Smith, one a conservative businessman, the other a professor of radical leanings.

Arising early one morning, Conservative Smith glances at the headlines, which feature the Government's latest incursions into the economy (whatever they may be), and groans: They are out to destroy the business system. As he reads the details of these Government rulings and forays, he is moved to reflect on the invasion of Government into every facet of private life. Even his breakfast is touched by its ubiquitous presence—the orange juice container, the wrapper on his loaf of bread, the tin that holds his coffee, all bear descriptive labels imposed by Government decree.

Indeed, as he goes about his day, it seems to Smith that it is impossible to escape from the presence of Government. The taxi he takes to Pennsylvania Station charges a fare set by Government. The train he boards for Washington (Government city) is owned and operated by the Government. Once in Washington, Smith learns that a proposed merger in which his company is interested will be forbidden by a Government ruling. Telephoning the news to New York at rates set by a Government agency, he decides to return immediately, boarding an aircraft whose route, maintenance, equipment, operating procedures, and fare have all been Government-determined. On the trip home Smith figures how much of his year-end bonus will go to the Government in taxes, ruefully calculating the rate at 50 percent: how can a man make any money, he asks, when he works as much for the Government as for himself?

Home again, he relaxes in his apartment, whose construction was partly subsidized by Government, and idly watches a Government-licensed television station dutifully complying with a Government regulation to devote a portion of its prime time to public-interest broadcasting. His son, who attends a Government-supported university, comes in to borrow the family's car, which has been designed to meet certain Government specifications. Before retiring, Smith looks over his mail, which includes a bill from the Government for the Social Security payments he must make for his maid. Switching off the lights, for which he has been paying at Government-established rates, he settles into his bed, from whose mattress dangles the Government-decreed tag ("Do Not Remove Under Penalty of Law"), and as he finally dozes off, he asks himself: "Is this still capitalism? God, no!"

This is the sort of scenario that delights the guardians of economic conservatism. But consider it again, this time from the viewpoint of our other Smith, of radical political leanings.

Shaking his head over the paper at breakfast (once again the Government has acted as a front for business), Smith also observes the compulsory labels on his foods, but reflects on how little faith one can repose in them, given the sorry record of the Food and Drug Administration's responsiveness to industry pressure. Paying his cab fare downtown, Radical Smith muses that the taxi industry is controlled by a public agency more ready to boost fares than to increase the number of licensed cabs. Boarding the Amtrak train, he recalls that the railroad was taken over by Government only as a last resort to shore up a sagging industry. Arriving in Government city, he is struck by the ease with which business executives communicate their views to the Government and the difficulty with which the "working man" communicates his views: could this be, he wonders, why the tax laws so outrageously favor the rich and propertied, why a national health insurance plan is still lacking, why wage incomes suffer but dividends rise, despite the worst depression since 1929?

During his rounds, Smith hears of the failure of his namesake to pull off the merger he was seeking. Radical Smith is not much impressed, because he knows that Conservative Smith's experience was the exception rather than the rule. Largely because of mergers, the top 100 industrial corporations today own a larger percentage of total corporate assets than did the top 200 industrial firms only twenty years ago. So, too, Smith is not so impressed by the Government regulation of the plane on which he flies home as by the fact that regulation has largely been used to suppress competition: not a single new trunk line has been authorized since regulation began in 1938. Again, Radical Smith does not worry about Conservative Smith's tax burden, because he knows that the top 1 percent of taxpayers (with incomes of roughly $50,000 and up) pay an average of only 26 percent of their total incomes, including capital gains, to the Internal Revenue Services. He would point out as well that the expensive apartment house in which the other Smith lives was built with money provided for "low-cost" housing that somehow got diverted into high-cost housing; that the safety specifications on Smith's car are generally regarded as inadequate, thanks to industry protestations; that the Social Security payments going to the maid are insufficient to support her above the poverty level, whereas the electric light rates established by Government were intended to provide utility companies with profits of about 10 percent on sales. "Is this capitalism?" asks Radical Smith. "Of course. What else?"

Thus both Smiths would impatiently dismiss the question, "Is this capitalism?," although each would answer it differently. Nevertheless, I think it is useful to pose the question in all seriousness. For I am inclined to think that neither the stereotyped conservative nor radical conceptions of capitalism shed enough light on the economic and political reality that surrounds us, much less on the destination toward which we may be headed.

Let me begin with the conservative's picture of

capitalism. Like the radical's, it is founded on what we might call a minimal structural definition: capitalism is an economic system in which the means of production—factories, farms, mines, etc.—are owned by private individuals or firms, and in which the primary method of distributing incomes is the competition of the marketplace. We shall have an opportunity later to discuss how useful this minimal definition is. But also like the radical, the conservative sees more in capitalism than a bare institutional structure. He also sees capitalism as a larger social system, but a social system with a particular (although usually unacknowledged) characteristic. This is its essentially static nature. By this the conservative does not rule out change, above all the change of economic improvement. But the change affects economic magnitudes and not social relationships. Capitalism is thus conceived as a dynamic economic process contained in a basically fixed social setting, especially with regard to its class differences.

We shall return to this vision of a fundamentally fixed society. But one disturbing trend bedevils the conservative's static conception of capitalism. It is the trend we have already noticed—the steadily growing presence of Government. From decade to decade, government looms ever larger in the economic framework. No wonder, then, that the conservative pictures the intrusion of government as disruptive—even subversive—of the stable social milieu that capitalism implies to him.

Has the steady entry of government meant the subversion of capitalism? Let us try to answer the question by dividing the long history of government intervention into three distinct, although overlapping, periods. The first can be traced back to colonial America and probably reached its heyday in the early to middle decades of the nineteenth century. This is the period when government intruded into the economy as a direct stimulus for economic expansion itself. It is the era during which federal and state money made possible the network of early roads, canals, and railroads (not to mention public schools) that played an important role in imparting the momentum of growth to the formative system. To be sure, it is difficult to measure exactly the contribution made by government, but it seems indisputable that undertakings such as the Erie Canal, the transcontinental railroads, or later the Panama Canal, were at least as important for the expansion of capitalism in their time as the federal highway system, the airline network, or the armaments industry have been for the growth of the economy in more recent times. Need I add that these examples testify that the role of the government as a propulsive force for economic expansion has certainly not come to an end?

A second period of government's relation to capitalism began after the Civil War, vastly accelerated during the New Deal, and is perhaps peaking in our own time. This is the phase during which the main form of government intervention appears in the proliferation of agencies such as the Interstate Commerce Commission, the Federal Trade Commission, the Federal Reserve System, and the alphabet array that arose under Franklin Roosevelt to supervise the operation of agriculture, the securities industry, utilities, and the like.

What was the common element in this new insinuation of government power? I think most historians would agree that it was the regulation of markets. In one manner or another, the new agencies sought to bring order to markets in which the competitive process was threatening to bankrupt an industry (farming), or to undermine its reliability (banking), or to demoralize its operations (utilities). Indeed, one of the insights that radical historians have given us is the recognition of the role played by leading businessmen in actively promoting regulation in order to stave off the cut-throat competition and other evils they were unable to police by themselves. In 1911 Judge Elbert Gary, the arch-conservative head of the United States Steel Corporation, actually told a dumfounded Congressional Committee that "I believe we must come to enforced publicity and government control . . . even as to prices, and, so far as I am concerned . . . I would be very glad if we knew exactly where we stand . . . and if we had some place where we could go, to a responsible governmental authority, and to say to them, 'Here are our facts and figures . . . now you tell us what we have the right to do and what prices we have the right to charge.' "*

Whatever the responsibility of the business community in originating the legislation designed to control its own operations, there is little doubt that, once enacted, the regulatory laws were used to stabilize industrial operations. Here we can witness the long

---

*Quoted in Gabriel Kolko, *The Triumph of Conservatism* (Glencoe, Ill.: The Free Press, 1963), p. 174.

solicitous history of ICC railroad rate-setting, or the aforementioned refusal of the CAB to license an additional competitive trunk line. This does not mean that businessmen have "liked" being regulated, or that regulation has not to some extent served the public as well as the private interest. But the history of regulation makes it difficult to contend that the power of government has been used to "destroy" any sector over which it was appointed to keep order. On the contrary, the evidence is overwhelming that regulation has been used mainly to protect the regulated sector against competition, from within or without, or to ameliorate abuses threatening to undermine it.

A third phase of government-business interaction opens with the New Deal and is still very much with us. This is the active use of central government's powers to bring the economy to an acceptable level of employment, growth, and welfare.

Of all changes in business-government relations, this is probably the one most attended with feelings of "socialistic" betrayal on the part of conservatives. Indeed, in the late 1930s the Veritas Society was founded at Harvard University to expunge the teaching of Keynesian economics from the curriculum. I suspect that the Society is now defunct, for with the general embrace of Keynesian principles by the Republican Party there is no longer any respectable opposition to the use of the government's fiscal and monetary powers to counteract a deficiency in aggregate demand, or to bring individual incomes above some minimum poverty line. How conservative—how conserving of the busi-

25

ness system—does not the New Deal look in retrospect!

But just as the dust has settled in this area of government intervention, it is stirred up in another, brought about by a condition that was quite unforeseen by Keynes—namely, the stubborn persistence of inflation despite the presence of a very high level of unemployment.

Many efforts have been made in various countries to control inflation—tightening the money supply, deliberately deflating the economy, applying wage and price controls, formulating a concerted "incomes policy." None has yet been successful. There seems to be a chronic and deep-seated pressure for rising prices built into the operations of contemporary capitalism—a pressure that I shall argue in the next chapter resides ultimately in a changed balance of power between capital and labor, tilting the balance in favor of the latter.

Whatever the differences in the attempted cures for inflation, there is a marked common feature to the responses to the problem. *In one manner or another, public responsibility for the working of the system has been extended.* The economic aims of government have now been broadened to include the attainment of socially acceptable levels of price stability. Moreover, just because the various measures so far tried have not succeeded, I believe the reach of government intervention will be forced to expand still further, probably through controls that cover not only prices and wages, but also dividends and profits. If, as I shall contend, inflation is basically an endemic consequence of the operation of the economic mechanism, what possible remedy is there other than the assertion of a political will over the unwanted outcome of that mechanism?

This is a diagnosis that is today advanced by only a few economists and advocated by still fewer, John Kenneth Galbraith being a principal exception. But I believe the number of adherents for extended government intervention will grow if the underlying condition continues to be intractable to milder medicines, as has been the case to date in every capitalist nation. Moreover, despite the general distaste with which controls are viewed today, I presume it will not come as a surprise if I declare that their eventual imposition will be accepted as a measure needed to save, not to destroy, the business system.

Is the conservative wholly wrong, then, in his conception of capitalism? Clearly, I think he is indeed mistaken with regard to the ''subversive'' intent of government. Yet, oddly enough, I believe the conservative is right in his underlying picture of capitalism as a static social system. But it is not the institutional framework—and certainly not the business-state relationship—that is static. It is the social core of the system, its structure of privilege.

The most obvious and important form of this privilege is the continuous creation and allocation of a highly disproportionate share of income to two groups within capitalist society—those who own substantial quantities of property and those who man the command posts within the business world. Capitalism has always rewarded these strata generously. Going back to 1910,

27

admittedly on the basis of somewhat shaky data, we find that the top 10 percent of income recipients, whose incomes were mainly derived from property and management, got just over one-third of the nation's total individual income. In recent years, the top 10 percent of family units received about thirty percent of all income. The change, if any, has been miniscule. Moreover, on the basis of much firmer data, it seems certain that the share of the top 10 percent has been unchanged since 1960.

Income statistics are deceptive, because changes in the tax laws cause high-income receivers to rearrange the manner in which they get income, exchanging outright compensation for capital gains, or causing large payments to be deferred into installments over future years. However, when examining more substantial data with respect to the ownership of wealth, we find that here too the irrefutable impression is one of stability rather than change. Estimates based on studies by Robert Lampman and others indicate that the share of private wealth held by the top 2 percent of all families declined from 33 percent in 1922 to 25 percent in 1949, but thereafter rose again to 32 percent in 1958. There is no evidence that the concentration of wealth has diminished since then.

The point of these well-known statistics is obvious. Despite fifty years of increased government intervention, supposedly "confiscatory" taxation, welfare statism, and the rest, nothing like a dramatic change has marked the distribution of income or wealth within American capitalism. This in no way denies that the system has generated a steadily rising standard of living for most of the population. But there remains a vast gulf between the quality of life of the "middle" classes—the 15 million-odd American families that enjoy, in the mid-1970s, incomes of more than about $10,000 but less than about $15,000—and the very small group of Americans—perhaps some 200,000 families in all —who enjoy an annual income of $100,000 or more. It is this stratum of privilege that capitalism protects, and whose persistence confirms, albeit from an unexpected angle, the conservative's view of capitalism as a system that grows but that does not fundamentally change.

Not surprisingly, the radical sees things from a diametrically opposite vantage point. Like the conservative, the radical also fastens on the pillars of private property and the market as the critical and distinctive institutions of capitalism. But unlike the conservative, who sees in these institutions the foundation for a static social system, the radical sees in them the source of a pervasive and ultimately irresistible dynamics.

In fact, to the radical the most striking attribute of capitalism is precisely its inherent tendency for revolutionary change, brought about by the irrepressible contradictions of its economic processes. The very problems that we have noted as generative of government intervention—the need to support and advance economic growth, the need to control markets, the need to assure a minimum of social provisioning, the need to repress inflation—appear to the radical as the outcome of the peculiar economic institutions and mechanisms of

29

capitalism, and the intervention of government therefore appears to him to be part of the inherent self-pre-
servative reaction of a system threatened with self-de-
struction.

I think the radical is essentially correct in this
diagnosis. Nonetheless, I find a weakness in the radical
view. It is a tendency to assume a subservience of the
political apparatus to the economic interests of the system—a subservience that ultimately defines too narrowly the independent power of government or the
independent shaping influence of social institutions. As
I have put it elsewhere, the radical view sees the economy as the engine and the government as the caboose in
the evolution of capitalism—indeed, perhaps of all
socio-economic systems. I believe the process is more
accurately likened to a train in which there are two
engines, one economic, one political, capable of pulling
in different directions as well as coordinating their efforts.

Only such a conception, I think, can help us understand the extraordinary variety of institutions that we
find when we survey the spectrum of countries with
private property and market bases. How else are we to
account for the differences between Japan, where the
large corporations guarantee lifetime employment to
their workers and where it is difficult to distinguish, at
the apex, government from business, and the United
States, where the indignities of unemployment are considered no part of a corporation's responsibilities and
where government and business intermingle but preserve their respective identities? How shall we explain

the severe taxation of upper-income groups in Norway with the easy enforcement of tax laws in Italy? How shall we understand the difference between Sweden, where the public sector, as such, is very small but the degree of public control over the economy is considerable, and France, where the public sector is formidable but its effectiveness small?

All these nations have economic structures that rest on private property and economic systems that depend on market forces. All display similar tendencies of instability, inflation, business concentration, and the like. But from nation to nation the degree and manner of public correction of these problems varies, largely as a consequence of differing capacities to create and maintain strong and effective political authorities willing to set themselves "against" as well as side by side with the business community.

This is a problem to which we shall return in due course. Here I wish to do no more than emphasize the existence of a political sphere whose composition, coherence, and will varies enormously from one capitalism to the next. The political engine in some capitalist economies is extremely powerful. In others it is weak. The deficiency of the radical view of capitalism lies in its failure to explain—or even to consider—this problem. The world of politics and power remains unexamined in the radical perspective, or worse, assumes the character of a passive accompaniment to changes in the economic structure. The tacit assumption is therefore that there can be no exercise of political power for ends that lie beyond those of

31

the maintenance of privilege. The possibility that the very preservation of society may require changes that will profoundly alter the social relationships of capitalism, or the still more heretical possibility that government may "detach" itself from the economic base and assert control for the ultimate purpose of preserving a system of political power, are not part of the radical scheme of things. Yet it is precisely such tendencies that I think underlie the long-term evolution of the system, in ways that we shall examine in the chapters to come.

But in this chapter we are considering only the immediate future—the next ten years or so of capitalist history. Is it possible to venture a general prognosis for this period? From what I have written, it should follow that the relationship between business and state will be affected primarily by the nature and severity of the difficulties generated by the economic workings of the system. And here I think we can discern three kinds of difficulties, present in varying degrees in all capitalist economies:

1. *There is the continued propensity of capitalism to develop generalized disorders that require government intervention.*
   Inflation is only the latest of these "macro" problems. Depression persists as a dangerous social malady. At the very least, these ills require a continuation of the existing levels of public intervention. If, as I shall maintain, in-

flation is deeply rooted in the economic system, or if the deflationary "cure" for inflation becomes worse than the disease, then we can expect further intervention along the lines I have indicated.

2. *There is a tendency to develop serious localized disorders.*

The near-breakdown of the mass transportation system in the United States, the near-collapse of the financial structure in Europe and the United States in the early 1970s, the near-insolvency of many cities at home and abroad, are all instances of recent "micro" failures within the economy. They have brought increasing government involvement in the rescue of the affected areas, for it is evident that railroads, large banks, or vital cities cannot go bankrupt without creating a vast wreckage. This is a consequence of an ever more tightly knit economic mechanism. I therefore suspect that the trend toward government ownership of unprofitable private activities, and responsibility for failing local public activities, will increase further in the future.

3. *There are the dangers imposed by a constricting environment.*

During the past few years, we have become aware of the possibility of overrunning our resource base before technological remedies can be found. There is also a growing unease over the damage that unconstrained industrial expansion works on the life-carrying capabilities of the planet. These new elements add an imperious force for the monitoring, direction, and, if needed, forceful suppression of economic activity. Much has been written about these environmental challenges, and I shall refer to them many times. I shall therefore say no more at this stage than to point to their obvious implications with respect to the extension of the government's role within the economic system.

Thus the general prognosis for the immediate future seems very clear. The next phase of capitalism must be an increasingly planned system, and the drift of business society will be toward a business-government state.

Once such a statement might have provoked general shocked disbelief. I doubt that it does today. A catechistic distaste for "planning" continues to be aired in the business press, especially in our country, but we find ample evidence that even American business leaders anticipate the establishment of a planned capitalist economy. Five years ago Thomas J. Watson of IBM was already calling for "national goal-setting and planning" before the New York Bond Club, and Robert Sarnoff of RCA was echoing his views before the National Industrial Conference Board. More recently we have seen the introduction of a bill calling for national economic planning under the joint sponsorship of Senators Hubert Humphrey and Jacob Javits. The bill is mild, calling for little more than the coordination of statistical information and the formulation of a coherent set of national and regional objectives over varying time spans. There is no provision for enforcement of these objectives, no mention of wage or price or dividend controls, no hint of a public supervision of private investment or a public regulation of wasteful consumer practices. But the bill is nonetheless significant for the change in attitude to which it testifies.

Ironically, the conservative opposition to planning, which sees this mild measure as the precursor to a network of ever more demanding and stringent controls, is probably correct. We shall inquire further into this trend in later chapters. *But what the conservatives fail to see is that there is no alternative to planning if capitalism is to be kept alive at all.*

For certainly the purpose behind the imposition of state regulation and control is to maintain that inertial core of institutions and privileges central to a business civilization. The prerogatives of many enterprises may have to be curtailed under a system of national planning, but the business framework, with its profit-generating capability, will be protected as long as it is possible to do so. I would suggest that the emerging economic structure of the near-term future will therefore be characterized by large, bureaucratic corporations, organized into a viable whole by a planning agency that attempts to reconcile the drive for business profits with the evident need to curtail activity in some areas and to encourage it in others. As part of this coordination of private and public activity, the planning agency will also seek to avoid disasters, either at the macro or micro level, that threaten the stability of the business system as a whole. Thus at one level of analysis, the drift into planning, as with previous enlargements of government presence, represents an effort to adapt the system of private property and market privilege to new dangers and challenges that might otherwise disrupt it fatally.

Yet from another perspective, planning is more than an adaptation of capitalism. No doubt corporations will have a major influence in the determination of the size and composition of the national plan. But to assume that the plan itself will remain nothing but the additive sum of private interests, or will always cater to the prerogatives of corporate elites, is to assume away the increasing gravity of the situation with which the national planning authority will have to deal. However much the market is allowed to function in the future, whatever degree of autonomy is left to the corporation manager, however disproportionately large his income, "business" in the planned state is apt to become more and more the civil service of the nation-state, providing the indispensable but essentially passive support that is today rendered to the business community by the functions of government. To put the matter as concretely as possible (and to choose a case that is already a harbinger of the future), whereas government in the first quarter of this century provided the underpinnings for the free exercise of whatever services the transportation industry found it profitable to provide, in the last quarter of this century the transportation industry will more and more provide the implementation for whatever transportation policy the government determines to be in the interest of national survival.

Business operation under this new dispensation takes on a different coloration. As the business world becomes merged with or submerged beneath a national economic state, the social responsibility of corporations or ministries becomes less and less distinguishable from that of government itself. This by no means solves the problem of responsible behavior, for we have learned that nationalization is no cure-all for the misbehavior of the corporation. Indeed, it may be more difficult to fix responsibility and accountability on large units that operate under the cloak of the public interest than on those that cannot pretend to more than a private interest. This raises the possibility that in the immediate future the most effective means of planning may be mixed productive sectors in which certain units are nationalized to serve as national policy setters, while the rest of the industry is left to fend for itself (and to earn a profit) in order to prevent the nationalized salient from becoming fossilized.

Will this then be "capitalism"? Will it still be recognizably a business civilization? Given the variety of adaptations that can be made to underlying changes in the economic structure, it is difficult to know what term to use. Certainly the advent of planning promises to change the *institutional* character of capitalism, perhaps as fundamentally as the change between the "atomistic" system of Adam Smith's day and the monopolistic system of our own. The degree to which it will alter the *inertial social core of privilege* remains more difficult to

37

predict, although we shall conjecture about it in the next chapter. Perhaps the historian of the future will need some new term to depict the impending state of affairs. More likely, I think, he will simply describe it as the era of planned capitalism—the era of transition between the still business-dominated system of our age and the state-dominated system of the future.

TWO

The Middle Distance

IT SEEMS TO me, although perhaps not to my readers, relatively easy to predict the general outlines of the "next phase" of capitalism—a phase that has already begun in our times. More difficult is to look further ahead—not into the very distant future, for there, as we shall see, I believe the prognosis is equally clear—but into the middle distance, say twenty-five to fifty years ahead.

Here the difficulty arises, strangely enough, from an excess of knowledge, as well as from a deficiency of it. Of course there is always the curtain of ignorance through which we cannot peer. But in the period of the middle range to which we address ourselves here, we have an additional handicap that greatly weakens our efforts to think cogently about the fate of the business system. For a disconcerting fact must be faced by anyone who presumes to discuss the outlook for capitalism with some semblance of confidence. It is that the two most persuasive predictions with regard to its middle-run future have both been tried and found wanting, and that we must therefore frame our hypotheses about that future without the support of theories that, explicitly or otherwise, provided the basis for our prognostications in the past.

The first of these two theories was never, perhaps,

41

dominant in the Western world, but it has always provided a powerful current of thought for those who opposed capitalism, and to some degree influenced the thinking of many who were favorably disposed toward it. It is the theory, Marxian in origin, that capitalism is an inherently self-destructive social order whose destination had been correctly foreseen by Marx when he wrote:

Along with the constantly diminishing number of the magnates of capital . . . grows the revolt of the working class, a class always increasing in numbers, and disciplined, united, organized by the very mechanism of the process of capitalist production itself.

The productive forces of society come into contradiction with the existing social relationships. . . . [A]n epoch of social revolution begins. With the change in the economic structure the whole vast superstructure is more or less rapidly transformed. [T]he knell of capitalist private property sounds. The expropriators are expropriated.*

I need hardly say that history has so far not confirmed this apocalyptic view. Capitalism teetered briefly in the United States and England in the 1930s, but it did not collapse; and with the exception of Russia, wherever capitalism underwent violent change, as in Germany and Italy, the direction of movement was to the Right, not to the Left. Even more disconcerting to the believer in the Marxian drama, when the storm of fascism had passed, capitalism reemerged in excellent health, as witness the remarkable postwar histories of Germany and Japan.

*Karl Marx, *Capital*, Vol. I, Ch. 32; Preface to *The Critique of Political Economy; Capital, op. cit.*

What happened to disconfirm the Marxian prognosis of the future of capitalism? Here we begin to encounter those new elements in our knowledge that make present-day prevision so difficult. The first such element is the realization that the present-day industrial working class is not revolutionary in its temper. As Ernest Nolte has written with regard to that once firmly held belief:

Rarely has a doctrine ever frightened so many people, endowed so many people with totally unknown confidence, as the doctrine of the class war of the revolutionary proletariat. Rarely has a doctrine ever had such an overwhelming success in its early stages, such a stubborn series of failure in its continuing realization.*

Why did the doctrine fail? The reasons are many. Primary, of course, is that the economic system did not collapse, so that the pressures of economic misery so unforgettably described by Marx were slowly alleviated. Next in importance is that the combined economic and technological pressures of an expansive capitalism did not serve to swell, but rather contracted the numbers of the proletariat, opening the way for many to join the ranks of white-collar workers. This is a development we shall trace more carefully in the next chapter. As a result, the political temper and social outlook of the working class has become progressively less ''proletarian'' and progressively more ''bourgeois'', destroying as a further consequence the unity and discipline that Marx had expected of his revolutionary class. Not least in this array of causes must be placed the

*Ernest Nolte, *Three Faces of Fascism* (New York: Mentor, 1969), p. 206.

disillusion that gradually attached itself to the idea of socialism, as the harsh realities of Stalinism dashed hopes that the end of capitalism would usher in an instant transition to a new classless society.

Yet, as I have already said, the apocalyptic view of capitalism, although very important in giving certitude to the outlook of those who adhered to it, was always the outlook of a minority. Hence its disconfirmation would seem to enhance the claims of another, more sanguine set of expectations with regard to the future of capitalism. But here we encounter the second disconcerting element of our recently gained knowledge. By way of highlighting its relationship to the previous apocalyptic view, I would call it the end of the belief in an ameliorative capitalism.

What I have in mind is not an assertion that capitalism cannot improve its performance, augment the provision of social services, or carry out a number of other reforms. My contention is much more fundamentally shaking, especially for those who hope that the future can be discerned simply by projecting the economic trends of the past. *It is that economic success does not guarantee social harmony.*

Of all the elements of knowledge gained in the present generation, I can think of none so radically challenging for the social theorist. Let me present as an instance the case of the United States. Had anyone in the 1930s been told that the U.S. gross national product in the mid-1970s would reach $1.5 trillion—effectively doubling, with all allowance for inflation, the per capita income of the majority of the population living in the 1930s—I am sure he would have felt safe in predicting an era of unprecedented social peace and goodwill.

Yet that enormous economic change has taken place, and social harmony has not resulted from it. Economic growth did not prove to be the great solvent for social difficulties. In the United States, the economic transformation from the conditions of the 1930s to those of the 1970s has not headed off racial violence, an explosion of juvenile disorders, a widespread decay in urban amenities, a serious deterioration in national morale. Indeed, growth has brought new problems, environmental and other. And this disturbing experience has not been confined to the United States. Unprecedented growth in France and Germany has not prevented outbreaks of disaffection in those countries, particularly among the young. Nor have Sweden or England or the Netherlands—all countries in which real living standards have vastly improved and in which special efforts have been made to lessen the economic and social distance between classes—been spared the expression of profound social discontents.

What lies behind this failure of economic success to bring social stability and contentment? We can only hazard a few guesses. One is that poverty, beyond a certain point, becomes a relative and not an absolute condition, so that despite growth, a feeling of deprivation remains to breed its ugly social consequences. Another is that each generation takes for granted the standard of living that it inherits and feels no debt of gratitude to the past, so that the psychic gains from growth are not cumulative. Even these guesses, however, many smack too much of economic determinism. The lesson of the past decades may simply confirm that there is a weakness in business civilization itself. Affluence does not buy morale, a sense of community, even a quiescent conformity. Indeed, it may only permit large numbers of people to express political and social dissatisfaction because they are no longer crushed by the burdens of the economic struggle. These are matters we shall examine again at the end of this book.

This inability of a "successful" capitalism to produce social harmony adds more than another neutral element of knowledge to our uncertainty with regard to the future. Rather, the lesson of the recent past adds a distinctly pessimistic note to offset the optimistic implications of the decline of the apocalyptic view of capitalism. For I think it is fair to say that the skepticism and lack of commitment of youth—not to mention the drug culture or the cry for participatory democracy—are uncongenial with, or destructive of those attitudes and behavior patterns on which a business civilization has traditionally rested. It is possible, in other words, that we stand at the threshold of an era in which deepseated changes in lifeways will undermine capitalism in a manner as fatal as the most dramatic proletarian revolution.

I have been discussing the failure of two stereotypic conceptions of the future in order to understand the reasons for our sense of insecurity in peering into the middle range. Formerly, like a motorist blinded in a dense fog, we thought we knew the general direction in which the road led, even though we could not see very far ahead. With the collapse of our picture of capitalism as a system leading with ineluctable momentum either to an apocalyptic or an ameliorative conclusion, we come to a halt, peering about us into the mist. Yet because we are forced to stop, we are in a position to do something a motorist cannot—namely, examine the ground on which we stand.

When we do examine the ground beneath us, I think we quickly discover one very important thing. The composition of this ground, which we call "capitalism," is considerably different from the idea of it that underlay both the apocalyptic and the ameliorative conceptions of the system. For in both the Marxian and the "liberal" views of capitalism, there was an important common belief. This was the primacy of the economic machinery of capitalism in setting the tone and temper of its political and social life. In the previous chapter I described some of the differences between the radical and conservative interpretations of capitalism, but I also called attention to their agreement on the structural properties of the system. Here let me emphasize a further point of agreement—namely, the precedence that both conservative and radical views accorded to the economic elements of capitalism over its political elements. In the radical view, we discussed this precedence, and its consequent disregard of politics as a possible independent force. This view was expressed most trenchantly in the stinging phrase from the *Communist Manifesto* that described government as the "executive committee of the bourgeoisie." In the conservative view, no such passive relationship was ever explicitly emphasized, but the philosophy of laissez faire nevertheless implicitly declared that the inherent economic tendencies within the system should be allowed to work themselves out with a minimum of political interference.

It is this conception of capitalism as a system in which the economic elements were expected to predominate over the political and social elements that now demands our critical scrutiny. To begin with, let us recognize that both views erected a stereotype of capitalism that ignored important aspects of reality. Despite the sting of the Marxian phrase, it was already clear from the early nineteenth century on that the "executive committee" was capable of very wide latitude in its task of attending to the interests of the ruling classes, particularly because those interests were often at odds with themselves, or ill-defined, or simply suicidal. Thus the concept of the executive committee failed to describe, much less to analyze, the lengths to which the governing apparatus could go in the interests of maintaining the underlying system of class privilege itself. On the other side of the ideological divide, the laissez fairists closed their eyes to the fact that the governing institutions have in fact continuously intervened into the economic system to maintain it in good working order.

Yet it is evident, as we examine the history of capitalism, particularly since World War II, that this general ascription of precedence to the economic machinery and passivity to the political machinery is no longer a valid description of things. We have already looked into the reasons behind this trend of affairs. Now let us see what this undeniable growth of a political presence does to our ability to foresee the trend of the system, once the immediate transition into planning is past.

One overriding implication immediately strikes us. It is that the rise of the political ''superstructure'' to a position of much greater equality with, and now indeed to a prospective position of superiority over, the economic mechanism adds still another element of uncertainty with regard to our view of the middle range. For whatever our beliefs in the adaptive capabilities of capitalism, whatever resilience or flexibility we accord to a business civilization under pressure, it is clear that our prediction must hinge mainly on the political and social, rather than the purely economic properties of the system.

It is entirely possible to maintain, for example, that ''Swedish'' capitalism will avoid serious disasters and maintain much of its present inertial core, whereas ''French'' or ''American'' capitalism will not. These different outcomes, however, are not likely to reside in differences in the severity of depressions, inflations, micro, or environmental disorders. Rather, they arrive from the unequal ability of these nations to call on reserves of tradition, machineries of administration, or sheer good fortunes of political life. Because we possess no predictive powers and none but the dimmest previsions with regard to these crucial matters, the ability to foretell the shape of the capitalist system in the middle range is even more obscured. No wonder, then, that prognosis over this range seems hopelessly difficult.

Are we left, then, with no sense of the shape of things ahead, beyond the conviction that political dispositions will become of far greater importance than the blind workings of economic mechanisms? I think we are not quite so handicapped as that. For along with the melting away of old certainties comes the gradual recognition of new trends and pressures. If we cannot easily foretell their outcomes, at least we can identify the nature of the coming strains and the challenges they will present.

The first of these may come as something of a surprise after so much talk of dysfunction and impending environmental constraint. For it is the problem posed by affluence—a matter little considered by economists, although I believe it underlies much of our present inflationary tendency, and portends much more serious difficulties for the future.

Affluence depends, of course, on increases in output, and may therefore seem to contradict the stress I have placed on the need to control growth. But I do not believe that the need to control growth will much affect the increase of affluence within the period of twenty-five to fifty years that we are considering. Environmental limits are likely to curtail *particular* outputs, to cause rearrangements of priorities, or to force shifts from private consumption to public consumption, such as from automobiles to buses and trains. Barring horrendous war, however, I do not think it is realistic to expect a general lowering of all incomes during this period.

More important, the affluence that I have in mind does not depend so much on the possession of private good as on the possession of rights and expectations with regard to income and economic security. For the effect of capitalist affluence has been not only to increase the material standard of its masses. It has also progressively eroded the foundation on which its market operations depended. This foundation, as both Karl Marx and Max Weber stressed, was the presence of a large body of propertyless workers who had nothing to sell but their labor power and who were forced to sell that labor as their only means of staying alive.

Forced labor in this sense—wage slavery in Marx's term—is still a major economic reality in most capitalist systems. But it is a steadily weakening one. All capitalist nations today provide various layers of economic security for those who cannot find work—security that is often inadequate to maintain an unemployed worker above a mean existence, but security that nonetheless removes the need for him or her to take any job at any price. The presence of unfilled jobs of menial kinds, both in industrial and service work, despite the existence of high unemployment, testifies to the fact that the pressure of importunate need is diminishing. I think it is plain that this pressure will continue to diminish, partly because another several decades of growth will enhance private affluence, partly because every indication points to increasing "social affluence" in the form of a wider and more substantial protection against private economic insecurity.

In the rise of this social affluence are to be found two sources of difficulty that will impinge on the political and economic framework of statist capitalism. The first we have already seen in the advent of inflation as a process that has affected every capitalist society. Many sources have contributed to this process—accidental ones, such as oil embargoes or failures of crops, "technical" ones, such as the overly rapid increase in the money supply, "power-centered" ones, such as the United States' international economic policy during the Vietnam war with its enormous addition to foreign bank reserves.

Yet, in addition to these undoubtedly puissant sources of inflation, we also find the steady rise of wages ahead of productivity—a rise especially marked in the areas of services, including not least municipal services. There are many explanations for this rise in wages, some of them tied to the other causes of inflation that we have mentioned. Yet I think that most observers would agree that ultimately the increase in wages reflects an ability of the working class to demand higher wages than in the past. The threat of a strike was once limited by the essentially short staying power of unemployed workers. Today, larger union treasuries apart, this staying power is greatly strengthened by the unemployment insurance—and, if need be, by the "welfare"—that are available in case of dire need. Thus the institutions of social affluence are gradually altering the balance of strength in favor of labor, and will continue to do so as social affluence increases.

I believe the endemic inflationary process of capitalism owes much of its persistence to this enhancement of the power of labor in a setting of affluence. There is, moreover, no automatic means to bring such a process under control save a harsh deflation or a government-enforced "social contract." The philosophy of a welfare state makes the adoption of harsh measures politically difficult, if not impossible, for an extended period of time; and the formation of a social contract requires the imposition of those political controls over the economy of which we spoke in the last chapter.

To these results of affluence I wish now to add another, equally relevant to the middle range of prognostication in which we are interested. This is the need to discover some new social discipline to provide a labor force willing to undertake the more distasteful jobs of society as the threshold of affluence rises. What can such a discipline be? Appeals to conscience and to patriotism, the import of "mercenaries" in the form of foreign workers (with all the political problems associated with the ingestion of a large foreign population), the use of troops, the intervention of public authority through the courts, the outright militarization or draft of labor are all possibilities. More than that, most of them have already been used, with greater or lesser success. From what we have described as the tendency of the private and social affluence of capitalism to rise, we can expect that recourse to such nonmarket means of providing a labor supply will become an ever more pressing issue for capitalism in the middle range of its future.

There is, perhaps, one long-term means of avoiding an extension of political power to assure the needed supply of labor. This would be the development of technology in general, and automation in particular, to the point where labor requirements would be vastly lessened. I believe that resource constraints will make such a massive mechanization of work extremely unlikely. More to the point, however, the replacement of labor by machinery would sever the connection between work and income that today assures—albeit none too satisfactorily—that all families have access to purchasing power. The radical curtailment of the work force would thus necessitate some other, nonmarket means of income distribution. Mechanization may therefore provide an imaginable remedy for the problem of labor mobilization, but only at the cost of further encouraging the extension of political authority into the economic process along a different route.

My second middle-range problem brings an abrupt change of focus. Up to this point I have been interested mainly in stressing the political and social variances among capitalisms. But now I want to emphasize a point of important resemblance. This is the common technology employed by capitalisms all over the world. I do not mean, of course, that there is one and only one way of making steel or producing paper. But just as we are more struck by the likeness of airports around the world than by their differences, so when we look at the factories or offices of capitalist societies that may differ widely in political and social institutions, we are struck by their common attributes, above all by their organization along lines of efficiency, mass production, more or less continuous flows of outputs.

From this socio-technological fact follow consequences of great importance. For the presence of a common technique imposes a common set of effects on the social superstructure of capitalism. The first of these is to be found in the hierarchical organization of work, and the subjection of the work force to a routine imposed by the need for "efficient" and continuous output. I do not doubt that this work process can be decentralized and democratized to some extent, as in the manner now being tried in Sweden. But I suspect that efforts to alter this process will not be able to proceed very far, in part because of the need to meet the competition of other, less humanely organized production units, and in part because these methods conflict with the engineering and "businesslike" mentality of the industrial system itself.

Second, and no less important, the presence of huge, coordinated production units requires administrative control mechanisms to guide and superintend the flow of work. These administrative supports are to be found in the first instance *within* the corporation, and now, more and more, as we have seen, outside the corporation, within the government. Thus industrial production itself becomes a source of much of the bureaucratic trend that we find in capitalist nations —partly to ensure the orderly progression of work, partly to ensure the dovetailing of outputs, partly to repair the inevitable miscalculations that threaten the stability of the interlocked system.

It is within this scaffolding of industrial bureaucracy that we find the origin of those new elites identified by many observers, myself included, as contenders for the command posts of the economy. The "technostructure" that advises, oversees, and carries out the orders of the present capitalist class is becoming an order whose potential for power already rivals that of their masters, much as was once the case with the merchant traders in feudal Europe. It seems likely, therefore, that a second general problem for capitalism in the middle range of the future will be a contest for power—not between capital and labor, but between capital and the scientific-technical elite, again akin to the struggle that marked the transition of the medieval order into early capitalism. I need hardly emphasize that the locus of this struggle also lies in the political, not in the economic, arena of capitalism; and that it may be decided differently in different capitalist countries.

My third challenge of the middle range future is again of a technological and scientific kind. It has to do with the need to establish effective social controls over technologies that hold the capacity for enormous social mischief.

Here I include not alone those familiar processes of combustion or industrial output that threaten us with pollution—I have already assumed that these immediate sources of damage will have to be curtailed or corrected. It is the far reach of science and technology that is at stake, a reach that we can expect to extend much further in the time span of our present concern. In this far reach we find the growing ability to perform genetic "engineering," to defer death through transplants, to affect the sex of unborn children, to condition behavior through drugs or electrodes, to alter the weather, to indulge in widespread personal surveillance, to affect attitudes by subliminal advertising or propaganda, and a host more. To control the effects of these technologies, to ration or perhaps prohibit their application, is likely to become a prime challenge for the civilization of capitalism in the next generations.

This is a task for which we are today almost totally unprepared. The blind encouragement of science and technology has achieved a degree of legitimacy comparable to that once accorded to the blind play of market forces. No capitalist nation has yet dared to exercise social censorship over the advance of science. In part this is because it is extremely difficult to distinguish the benign from the malign effects of a technological change; in part because no nation dares sacrifice the military advantages that may accrue from unrestrained scientific work; in part because the assumption is still unchallenged that "science" is inherently an activity whose ultimate effects are good for mankind; in part because science and technology are prime sources of profit. Whether a business civilization will overcome its inhibitions with respect to the control of science is problematical; but then, as we shall see, whether a noncapitalist society would fare better in this regard is equally open to question.

This last consideration brings us to the final—and I think firmest—generalization that can be risked with respect to problems of the middle future. *It is that its problems are at least as much rooted in the nature of industrial society as they are rooted in capitalism proper.* For it is not only capitalist societies but socialist ones that must cope with the problem of marshalling a labor force under conditions of growing affluence (including in that term, let us emphasize, the assured provision of basic needs). It is certainly not capitalism alone that will be marked by the growth of bureaucracies organized to oversee the steady flow of production. Scientific and technical elites have already appeared in the power structures of socialism as they have in those of capitalism. And the worship of science and technology is at least as much in evidence in the present spectrum of advanced socialist nations as it is within the spectrum of capitalist ones. Thus it does not seem unrealistic to think of the middle range as a time of "trans-systemic challenges" rooted in the industrial nature of society rather than as a series of challenges specific to capitalism alone.

This is not to say that capitalist and socialist nations will not have their general differences in coping with common problems. The capitalist group brings with it the obsolete privileges of inherited wealth, of acquisitiveness as a dubious source of social morale, of the clash between a "business" outlook of decreasing relevance and a technical-planning outlook of uncertain strength. On the other hand, these nations generally enjoy parliamentary forms of government that, if they withstand the transition through planning, may provide useful channels for social adaptation.

On the socialist side we find the advantage of economic systems stripped of the mystique of "private ownership" and the presumed legitimacy and superiority of the workings of the market. On the negative side is the cumbersomeness of their present planning machinery, their failure to develop incentives superior to capitalism, and above all, their still restrictive political attitudes.

In the middle run, then, it seems plausible that the economic institutions of socialism may prove superior to those of planned capitalism, whereas the political institutions of capitalism may present advantages over those of socialism (as matters now stand). The hope, of course, is that we can combine the two—welding the best of socialist economic practice with the best of liberal capitalist political practice. I have no hesitation in setting such a goal as that for which we should strive in the coming middle period. Whether it will be attainable cannot be predicted.

THREE

"Postindustrial" Capitalism

THE LAST CHAPTER ended on the question of whether the future would be dominated by problems peculiar to "capitalism" or "socialism," or by problems characterized by an industrial system. But there remains a question to which we have not yet addressed ourselves. It is whether industrialism is a proper description of the society of the future. Are we not moving in a direction that is called "post-industrial"—a direction in which basic economic relationships will be as different from those of today as those today differ from those of the preindustrial era?

It must be apparent from the quotation marks with which I enclose the word *postindustrial* in the title that I view this contention with considerable skepticism. Yet I do not think it is wholly wrong. Hence I suggest that we explore this rather voguish term both critically and sympathetically, to see what light it may throw on the problem of the future.

Let me start by examining three different meanings that are commonly attached to the word postindustrial:

1. *A postindustrial society will be one in which a preponderance of economic activity is located in the "tertiary" (or service) sector of the economy.*

This definition of postindustrialism calls attention

63

to a shift in the distribution of occupations whose beginnings can be traced at least as far back as the nineteenth century. As the history of every industrialized country indicates, the proportion of the labor force employed in agriculture has shrunk to a very small fraction of the labor force: in the United States today only about 4 percent of the civilian working force is to be found on the farm, and this includes a considerable residue of subsistence part-time farmers. Meanwhile, the industrial "core," comprising manufacturing, mining, and construction plus transportation and utilities, has stabilized at about one-third of the work force.* The remainder of the population, approaching two-thirds of the working force, is to be found in that potpourri of trades that produce "final" services, such as doctors' or teachers' or police officers' ministrations, financial or selling activity, catering, caretaking, etc.

From one industrial nation to another, the magnitude of these proportions varies, but the drift is visible in all, as the table opposite shows.

Thus the advent of a postindustrial society, marked by a shift in the distribution of occupations, can be amply demonstrated by the data. Nevertheless, a few cautionary remarks are in order here. First, let us note that the industrial sector has not been the source of the main change in the profile of employment. Although the percentage of industrial employment has declined slightly in France and England during the last decades, in Germany the percentage is unchanged, and in the

*Transportation and utilities are often grouped under "services." I include them in the industrial core because of their crucial importance in the production of manufactures.

Percentage Distribution of Employed Workers

		Agriculture	Industry	Service
United States	1900	38	38	24
	1950	12	33	55
	1972	4	32	64
France	1950	35	45	20
	1970	17	39	44
West Germany	1950	24	48	28
	1968	10	48	42
United Kingdom	1950	6	56	39
	1970	4	45	50

[SOURCE: Bureau of Census; OECD]

United States, *over a period of seventy years,* the decline has been small. The great sectoral transformation of our times, in other words, has not been so much a shift from industry to service as a shift from agricultural to service tasks.

In addition, we must note that some part of the rise in service employment represents the transfer of certain kinds of work from the unpaid household sector to the monetized commercial world. The rise in female labor participation (in the United States) from 18 percent of all females of working age in 1890 to about 40 percent today has brought as a consequence the illusion of a rise in service "employment," as tasks that were formerly done at home, invisible to the eye of the statistician, emerged onto the marketplace. The growth of such service industries as laundering and cleaning, restaurants, the professional care of the aged, even some "welfare," represent instances of a semispurious inflation of the growth of "employment" in these industries.

These caveats and distinctions are important to bear in mind when we use the shift in occupation as the basis for speculations about the implications of a postindustrial era. For presumably the importance of the employment shift for a postindustrial society is that a change in occupational habitat will bring new social experiences and needs. Without in any way challenging that supposition, let me warn against the misconception of that change as a massive emigration away from industrial work. Nothing of that kind is visible. The factory worker—the key *dramatis persona* of the Marxian drama—continues to account for approximately the same proportion of the total work experience of the community. Nonagricultural blue-collar work as a whole constituted a quarter of the labor force in 1900 and a third of it in the 1970s, the main changes taking place *within* this group as unskilled occupations gave way to "semiskilled". Thus, if a postindustrial society in fact represents a new stage of socio-economic relationships, the cause must be sought elsewhere than in the disappearance of the industrial sector as a milieu for work.*

2. *A postindustrial society will depend for its growth on "qualitative" rather than "quantitative" factors.*

*Since I wrote these words, I have been impressed with the work of Harry Braverman, *Labor and Monopoly Capital* (New York: Monthly Review Press, 1974). Braverman argues convincingly that much of the work in the service sector is indistinguishable, in terms of rhythms, demands, skills, pacing, or monotony, from work in the industrial sector. Indeed, he argues that the percentage of the population who are "workers" in the Marxian sense of being reduced to a dependency on wages has risen from 50 percent of the labor force in 1900 to about 70 percent today.

Here is a second meaning to the word postindustrial that calls our attention to numerous studies showing that "knowledge" has played an ever-rising part in promoting economic growth, compared with mere increases in the size of the labor force or the quantity of capital. Drawing on work by Edward Denison, we may generalize for the United States that for the two decades prior to 1929, increases in the quantity of capital and labor together accounted for about two-thirds of our increase in output, whereas in the decades 1929–1959 increases in the quantities of labor and capital accounted for less than half of our growth. Conversely, improved education and training, which were credited with only 13 percent of growth in the earlier period, appear to have been the source of more than twice that growth in the later period. Finally, improved technology—which is, after all, only the concrete application of knowledge—rose from 12 percent of the causes of growth to 20 percent in the same two periods.

These proportions also differ from nation to nation, as has been shown in studies of Western European nations, but the direction of change, as in the case of the migration of labor from sector to sector, is the same throughout. In sum, there is no doubt that a statistical examination of growth patterns among industrialized nations reveals a steadily increasing importance of "knowledge-related" inputs and a corresponding decline in increase in brute "labor power" or sheer quantities of technically unchanged capital (for example, the addition of more railroad tracks or roads).

As in the case of the definition of postindustrialism

that emphasizes the shift in the locus of employment, I do not want to denigrate the importance that has been attached to "human capital." Nonetheless, as before, it is important that we scrutinize this characterization of postindustrialism with a certain reserve. For when we do so, we encounter some unsettling considerations.

First, as we have all come to realize, the meaning of growth is both ill-defined and elusive. Between that collection of often arbitrary measured outputs called "gross national product" and any operational concept of "welfare" lies a wide and perhaps unbridgeable chasm. Hence much of the "growth" to which modern knowledge seems to contribute may be of little or no significance for human well-being: armaments, space exploration, and pollution-generating production at one extreme; frivolous gadgetry, style changes, and pollution-absorbing technology at the other—the one extreme producing deleterious or dangerous growth, the other illusory or defensive "growth." In a word, the *quality* of the growth of a postindustrial society must be compared with that of an industrial society before we can discuss the rise of knowledge-inputs as a cause for celebration.

Second, before looking for the implications of a shift toward a knowledge-input economy, it behooves us to inquire further into the meaning of knowledge itself. This brings us to the ways in which knowledge "input" is measured. One of these ways is by taking account of the rise in research and development expenditures, which have grown from roughly $1 billion per year at the end of World War I to a level of about $28 billion in the early 1970s. This enormous increase has led many observers to conclude that we have now "institutionalized" the process of scientific discovery and application, thereby radically changing the nature of the propulsive forces within the economy. More skeptical observers have noted that (inflation aside) research and development figures in the later years are swollen by the growing tendency to include routine testing or marketing procedures within the category of "research." The actual amount going for basic research in new industrial products for 1966 is estimated to be not $20 billion, but $1 billion.

In addition, a study by Jewkes, Sawers, and Stillerman* throws considerable doubt on the effectiveness of "institutional" invention. Rather, the evidence is that the preponderance of the important technological or scientific advances of this century has been made by individuals or small firms. Thus there is some reason to regard the "institutionalized" generation of knowledge characteristic of a postindustrial society as of much less significance than might at first appear.

A last caveat with respect to the supposed knowledge revolution applies to the rise in the "quantity" of education embodied in the work force. Measured by the conventional criteria of man-years of schooling, there is no doubt that this quantity has increased markedly. Only 6 percent of the population aged 17 were high school graduates in 1900, whereas nearly 80 percent had completed high school in 1970. Equally dramatic,

*John Jewkes, David Sawers, and Richard Stillerman, *The Sources of Invention* (New York: Norton, 1970).

whereas only 4 percent of the population aged 18 to 21 was enrolled in college at the turn of the century, today well over half this age group has begun higher education.

No one can gainsay this change which, like the change in the occupational tasks of labor, surely augurs new outlooks, experiences, and expectations for the labor force. To this matter we shall return. But it would be hasty to jump from the fact of a larger "quantity" of education bestowed upon the labor force to the conclusion that the stock of "knowledge" of society has increased in like degree. For along with the increased training undergone by the labor force has come an increase in the compartmentalization and specialization of its knowledge, best exemplified by comparing the wide-ranging capabilities of the nineteenth-century farmer with the much more narrowly defined work capabilities of the twentieth-century office clerk. To put the matter differently, we cannot assume that a postindustrial society will be one in which the general level of understanding is raised along with the general level of formal education. Insofar as formal education is devoted to exposing the student to the broad vistas of history, the social and natural sciences, etc., one kind of understanding is undoubtedly increased. In that sense, the citizen of a postindustrial society should be not only "better educated" but should really better understand the natural sciences or human behavior, *considered as abstractions*, than did his counterpart in industrial or preindustrial society.

70

At a less abstract level, however, the gain is much smaller. Indeed, within that very important branch of social knowledge concerned with the practical operation of the technology of production, what seems likely to mark a postindustrial society is a marked *decrease* in the ability of the individual to perform work outside his trained specialty—witness our helplessness in the face of a broken utensil, vehicle, electrical system, or plumbing fixture, compared with the versatility of the farmer or preindustrial artisan, proverbially jack of all trades even if master of none.

3. *A postindustrial society can also be regarded as a "postcapitalist" society—that is, as a system in which the traditional problems of capitalism will give way to a new set of problems related to the altered organizational structure of a postindustrial world.*

As with the previous visions of a postindustrial system, I think there is a core of truth in this view. The bitter class divisions endemic to capitalism in the late nineteenth and early twentieth centuries have yielded—and until growth ceases, are likely to continue to yield—to a society of much greater economic (although not necessarily social or political) consensus. The "welfare" state, however inadequate in actuality, is now a generally accepted model for all industrial societies, bringing with it a considerable degree of "socialism" in the form of guaranteed incomes, family allowances, public health assurance, educational access for low income groups, and the like. The extreme con-

71

sequences of a failure in aggregate demand have been tempered if not corrected by the growth of a public sector. As a result of these and still other changes, as we have seen, a "revolutionary" proletariat has failed to materialize.

Thus there are cogent reasons for thinking of a postindustrial society as one that may differ in significant ways from the economic performance of the industrial capitalism to which it will be successor. Nonetheless, as before, it is wise to look for continuities as well as differences in seeking to delineate the nature of the new socio-economic environment.

The first of these continuities is a trend to which we have already called attention. It is the slow, irregular, but apparently irreversible trend toward business concentration. To vary the figures given before, we might note that the top 200 firms in 1968 controlled as large a fraction of total corporate assets as did the top 1,000 firms in 1941. Economic society in our times is strikingly characterized by a small number of very large and powerful firms and a very large number of generally small and weak firms.

The development of a postindustrial configuration of employment or education does not seem likely to undo this characteristic of modern industrial systems. Rather, it seems probable that the concentration process will now proceed rapidly in the burgeoning service sector, where significant inroads have already been made. We tend to picture the service sector as comprised of large numbers of independent proprietors (lawyers, self-employed, one-man enterprises); but in fact a considerable proportion of employment in this sector is already provided by monopolistic or oligopolistic units. Of roughly 44 million people employed in the service sector in the early 1970s, 13 million were in federal, state, and local government, 15 million in trade, and 4 million in finance. By comparison with the manufacturing sector these are all relatively unconcentrated industries, but in terms of the absolute size of units, the large firm with its bureaucratic organization is increasingly evident. Of 465,000 corporations in trade, for example, a mere 29 retail chains control a fifth of all assets; the predominance of large banks and insurance companies is well known (the top fifty banks account for about one-third of all banking employment, the top fifty insurance companies for about half of all insurance employees).

Thus the organizational character of industrial capitalism, with its hierarchies, its bureaucracies, and above all, its trend toward concentrated economic power, seems likely to continue in postindustrial society. It is reasonable to assume that along with this continued concentration of economic power will continue the concentration of personal fortunes and incomes also characteristic of industrial capitalism.

All these elements suggest that whatever else we may say about the postindustrial future, we should consider it as a stage of capitalism and not as a decisive step beyond capitalism. This is particularly the case when we consider again those tendencies within capitalism that point in the near future to planning, and in the middle future to the emergence of trans-systemic problems of industrialism.

We have discussed three primary attributes of a "postindustrial" system: a shift of work location from agricultural to service tasks; an increase in the role of "knowledge"; a decrease in the polarized class relations of nineteenth-century capitalism. Is there anything in these developments that leads us to change our expectations with regard to the future? On the contrary, do not the decline of a self-sufficient agricultural sector, the increase in the exposure to education, and the diminution of class tensions all enhance the need for, or the receptivity to, planning? Moreover, do any of these developments throw into the question the difficulties of labor recruitment in an affluent social setting, the growth of bureaucracies within and around the economic process, or the challenge of coping with dangerous scientific techniques? I think not.

Shall we then dismiss the idea of a postindustrial society? That is not my intent, either. For there are significant implications within the trends we have been examining that will help us understand the pressures on capitalism in the middle range, where its "postindustrial" elements will be much more evident than they are today.

The first of these trends is the increasing importance of the service sector within the advanced economies of capitalism or socialism. I have taken issue with the misconception of this trend that presumes service occupations to have swelled at the expense of industrial rather than agricultural tasks, but I have no quarrel with the patent fact that the service area is increasingly the main occupational locus for employment. Now, when we are looking for indications of change, I think we should emphasize one aspect of this new location that is not usually pointed out. It is that the swelling of the service sector increases the vulnerability of the economy to the threat of labor stoppage.

Societies have, of course, always been vulnerable to work stoppages that lasted very long. But in the past this vulnerability was cushioned by the presence of inventories on which industry or the public could exist for a considerable period. Indeed, typically before the outbreak of a strike in the coal mines or the steel mills, customers of those industries bought supplies well in advance of needs so that production could continue unhindered while the strike was in progress.

The shift of society's activities in the direction of services lessens that margin of safety. Unlike goods, there is no way of stockpiling services. And whereas not every service is essential to the operation of an economy, in an urbanized setting more and more service occupations become capable of inflicting substantial damage if they are not regularly performed: recall the extraordinary interruption of economic life caused a few years ago by the brief strike of flight controllers; the much more serious threats to health and safety that have resulted from strikes of garbage collectors; and the disturbance to the social peace when teachers strike and children are unable to attend school.

As these instances also suggest, society cannot allow the resolution of strikes in the service sector to be settled in a leisurely way. Emergency bargaining sessions, immediate intervention by state and federal authorities, are unavoidable when the prospect of a protracted work stoppage holds dangers of immediate social disarray, unlike the delayed disruptions that attend a diminution of physical output. All this suggests, of course, yet another reason for the intensification of government intervention that we have described as the next phase of capitalism. The shift to services, like the rise of social affluence, adds to the "disruptive" power of labor, thereby further undermining the efficacy of the market mechanism and further encouraging the development of a planned economic system.

The second novel attribute of a postindustrial system is its emphasis on education. One effect of this emphasis is to change the conception of "work," identifying it more and more with tasks that resemble those of the classroom—writing, calculating, personnel-related activities—rather than material production. But there is another aspect that also deserves to be recognized. It is the likelihood that a society used to the security of an educational environment will expect a continuation of that security after school. A young man or woman who has been relieved of virtually all economic necessity until the age of 21 or even 25 is reared in an environment in which some sort of economic provision, even if at a frugal level, is taken for granted. Thus we should expect that the setting of a postindustrial society will inculcate strong feelings that work is not a scarce privilege, but a basic right—the normal reward for having completed the long training that society has enjoyed. Here is, therefore, an institutionally grounded basis for those feelings of "entitlement" that can be identified as characteristic of social affluence.

Last, let us turn to the contention that a postindustrial society implies some form of advance beyond the crude class conflict of industrial capitalism. We shall have reason, in the final chapter of this book, to conclude that this suppression of class differences is not likely to ensure in the face of the long-run challenges that we shall discuss. But it is entirely possible for a period of consensus to prevail during the range of the middle future, assuming that the political processes of capitalism have dealt in a satisfactory manner with the various problems that we have foreseen.

This ever-present importance of political action, to which we now revert once again, does, however, give additional significance to the idea of a postindustrial society. For the emergence of political decision making above the automatic workings of the market has a relevance to the period of the middle range on which we are focusing our attention. This is a characteristic of that age to which Adolph Lowe has given the title "the end of social fatalism."* By this title, Lowe describes the arrival of a new historic epoch in which the blows of social events—even the catastrophies of nature—are no longer passively accepted as the outcome of processes over which mankind has no control. Rather, they are

*Adolph Lowe, "Is Present Day Higher Education Still Relevant?", *Social Research,* Fall 1971.

seen as events that can be averted, forestalled, directed. More and more self-consciously, in other words, man "makes himself," embracing within the sphere of things over which he seeks to exert command a wider and wider portion of the universe, and above all, the social universe.

This exertion of active control in place of passive submission corresponds directly with the elevation of the political will over the blind interplay of economic forces. Economic momentum may still provide the motive force that bears against institutional structures or natural constraints, but less and less do the strata of society, high or low, stand prepared to let economic momentum work its way unimpeded. In a manner of speaking, postindustrial society thus becomes that period of economic history in which men make their boldest attempt to escape from the thralldom of social forces over which they hitherto exercised no control. Although hindered by the social baggage of the past in both capitalist and socialist state economies, the period of the middle future will be more and more characterized by the assertion of political mastery. To act is not necessarily to act wisely, and the exercise of political will in the middle-range future holds possibilities for terrible disasters. Nonetheless, it also represents a step in the liberation of mankind from the worst of all thralldoms—the submissive obedience to forces beyond understanding or question.

FOUR

Capitalism and the Multinational Corporation

THUS FAR WE have been considering the theme of tension between the economic forces and the political structures of capitalism as if the struggle could be fully considered within the confines of a single nation, or of a group of capitalist nations, with little or no relation to the rest of the world. This is clearly an inadequate representation of the problem. For the evolution of capitalism must contend with forces that impinge on it from other areas of the world, much of which is not capitalist, and it must also take into account the international expansion of capitalism itself—the transnational thrust that, from earliest times, has been a prime attribute of a business civilization.

This consideration of the international aspects of our problem requires that two additional elements be added to our analysis. The first of these—the relation of the capitalist civilization to the vast, formerly passive, areas of the underdeveloped world—we shall postpone until our final chapter. But the second element calls for consideration here. One of the most dramatic changes in the capitalist sphere has been the rise of an extraordinary new mechanism for the transmission of the capitalist impulse abroad. This is the advent of the multinational corporation with its extension of business activity beyond the boundaries of the nation-state itself.

A striking aspect of this multinationalization of economic activity has been the impetus given to the growth of already giant corporations. But there is implicit in the development of these immense, globe-straddling enterprises more than just an increase in size. What the multinationals promise—or threaten—is a development of great importance for capitalism. It is nothing less than the possible replacement of the nation-state by the international corporation as the chief organizing structure of the future.

This is the main question to which this chapter will be addressed. But before we proceed further, we had better clarify exactly what we mean by the term "multinational corporation." As an introduction to the subject, let me offer this description of a modern multinational—PepsiCo—by its president:

PepsiCo (operates) in 114 countries. Its most familiar product is bottled in 512 plants outside the United States. Production and distribution facilities in almost every country are owned by nationals of those countries. Regional managers may come from the area in question—or from some other part of the world—Frenchmen, Englishmen, Latin Americans—not necessarily from the United States. In the Philippines, where PepsiCo is about the twelfth largest taxpayer, the whole operation has only two persons from the home office. The company is multinational as far as employment, operations, manufacturing and marketing are concerned, and a good part of the operating management and plant ownership abroad is also multinational.*

*In *World Business*, Courtney Brown, ed. (New York: Macmillan, 1970), pp. 258–259.

We shall come back to certain aspects of this multinational operation—one suspects, for example, that the two Americans in the Philippine office are not office boys. But the essence of the matter is that PepsiCo no longer exports Pepsi-Cola to, say, Mexico. *It produces it there.* And precisely this same internationalization of production is to be found in IBM, General Motors, Ford, Standard Oil, and so on down the hierarchy of American corporate enterprise. I do not wish to imply that every big company is multinational. But we do know that 62 of the top 100 firms have production facilities in at least six foreign countries, and that 71 of the top 126 industrial corporations (for which data could be obtained) averaged one-third of their employment abroad as of the late 1960s.*

This is probably a considerable *under*estimate of the extent of multinationality of the top industrials, although it is wise to emphasize our ignorance concerning the multinational phenomenon itself. Consider, for example, the basic question of the value of the direct foreign investment—the plant and equipment, not the portfolios—owned by American enterprises. Our knowledge of the extent of this direct investment largely rests on a Commerce Department survey conducted in 1966. This survey collected data on 3,400 parent companies and 23,000 foreign affiliates. But efforts to enlarge and update that survey, now sadly out of date, have been systematically impeded. A government questionnaire sent to 500 companies in 1970 elicited only

*Cf. Kenneth Simmonds in *World Business,* ed. Courtney Brown, (New York: Macmillan, 1970), pp. 48–49.

298 responses. A more recent effort to discover some of
the missing facts was severely truncated by the opposition of a committee of government representatives to
questions that would invade the "privacy" of corporate
life.

Hence some of the most important information
required to assess the place of the multinationals in the
world economy remains fragmentary or incomplete.
We do not accurately know their capital outlays, their
research and development expenditures, their foreign-
based employment, the trade relationships between parent corporations and affiliates, or their full stockhold-
ings in local companies. Let me add that if American
data are inadequate, the statistical information obtained
by other nations on their multinational enterprises is far
worse. Many of the foreign multinationals maintain two
sets of books, one for the tax collector, another for
themselves, and most European countries do not even
have the staffs to compile the inaccurate statistics available from the "official" (i.e., tax-collector) books.

So we begin in a shadowy land of dubious facts.
According to these facts (based largely on projections
from the 1966 survey), the book value of American
foreign direct investment was $78 billion in 1970 and is
likely well over $100 billion in the mid-1970s. In round
numbers this compares with total assets (*including*
foreign assets) of a little over $500 billion for the top
1,000 industrial corporations in America in 1973—we
have no corresponding figures for, let us say, Sweden or
the Netherlands or Switzerland.

We have still less reliable data when we try to

estimate the sales of U.S. manufacturing affiliates abroad. The estimates we use are based mainly on guesses about how much output each dollar of investment is likely to generate. Working on this basis, the Commerce Department places the value of overseas production—not, remember, exports from the United States, but "American" goods produced abroad—at $90 billion in 1970. Assuming that sales abroad have been growing in accordance with past trends, this would put the value of American foreign production in the mid-seventies at perhaps $125 billion. Again by way of comparison, total sales (domestic plus foreign) of the top 1,000 manufacturing companies are something over $600 billion, as of 1973.

This seems clear enough. At a first glance we can locate a second "American" economy, scattered around the globe (although mainly concentrated in the European industrial market and the Near East oil market), which is about a quarter as big as the "home" economy.

First glances are, however, notoriously unreliable. For example, the value of American assets abroad includes $22 billion of assets in the petroleum industry, as of 1970. The marketable value of that portion of those assets represented by oil reserves is now much larger than in 1970—or is it much *smaller,* because the oil now "belongs" to the nations under whose sands it lies in a much more decisive fashion than in 1970? Another example: what about the banks that play so critical a role in supporting the growth of overseas enterprise? Any appraisal of the extent of multinationalism should take into account that foreign deposits in the nine biggest U.S. banks have risen from less than 30 percent of their total deposits in the late 1960s to over 66 percent in 1975, and that the total number of foreign locations for the twenty largest U.S. banks rose from 211 to 627 over the same period. But this information also escapes the standard measurement of the extent of multinational wealth.

So we begin with uncertainty about the true size of the multinational sphere. But we do know, with a fair degree of certainty, that the sphere is expanding very rapidly. Industrial sales abroad, to judge by the fragmentary data we possess, have been growing twice as fast as sales at home. So has the flow of capital into new investments abroad—in 1957 American companies invested about 10 cents abroad for every dollar of investment at home; today (at least until the recent depression) they are investing 25 cents. Total profits earned on operations abroad have risen from 25 percent of total profits at home in 1966 to 40 percent in 1970.

Furthermore, European and Japanese multinational firms are also accelerating their rate of growth. On the basis of past trends, these non-American multinationals are probably expanding even faster than U.S. firms. According to the estimates of Karl P. Savant of the University of Pennsylvania, about a quarter of world marketable output was attributable to the multinationals in 1968, and this share will rise to a third by the end of the 1970s and to over 50 percent by the last decade of this century.

These findings immediately indicate one aspect of

the multinational phenomenon. It is the challenge to the traditional sovereignty of capitalist nation-states offered by enterprises capable of shifting their assets and their production policies in ways that may seriously impinge on the ability of their home countries to pursue a self-determined economic policy. Multinational companies can, for example, offset the effect of stringent labor laws in one country by locating production facilities in other, more obliging countries. They can annul the intent of national foreign exchange policies by transferring profits from their overseas operations to their home countries or vice versa. They can juggle their profits by arbitrary pricing arrangements that magnify the profitability of operations in low-tax areas and that minimize it in high-tax areas: the oil companies' pricing policies have been notorious in this regard. Not least, they may concert their economic power with the political or military power of their home governments, as in the case of IT&T in Chile, or conceivably, they may deploy their economic power in ways that are contrary to the political designs of their home countries.

We shall revert to these difficult challenges later. But there is also a larger issue posed by the emergence of the multinationals. It is their tacit challenge to the nation-state itself as the irreducible "unit" of political economy. To some observers, such as Richard Barnet and Ronald Müller, these immense companies constitute "the most powerful human organization(s) yet devised for colonizing the future."* In place of the sprawling and inefficient nation-states that interpose

*Richard Barnet and Ronald Müller, *Global Reach* (New York: Simon & Schuster, 1974), p. 363.

their arbitrary and irregular boundaries over the globe, the multinationals offer the vision of world production organized along "transnational" lines designed to promote efficiency and technical superiority. They appear, therefore, to the archaic nation-state, what the nation-state itself was to the disorganized crazy-quilt of feudal autarchy. Already bigger and more powerful, in financial terms, than any but the largest nations, they suggest that capitalist enterprise, freed from the confines of its cramping national borders, will find in its multinational existence the organizational form required for its survival.

If this contention is true, it would profoundly alter our previous assessment of the survival capacities of a business civilization. But is it true? The impressive reach of multinational power does indeed suggest that some great sea change is underway. But here is where the picture becomes obscure and confusing. Consider, to begin with, the following thumbnail description of the multinational economy whose salient features we have been examining:

1. The concentration of production and capital has developed to such a high degree that it has created monopolies that play a decisive role in international economic life.

2. Bank capital has merged with industrial capital to create a financial "oligarchy."

3. The export of capital, as distinguished from the export of commodities, has become of crucial importance.

4. International cartels, or oligopolistic combines, have effectively divided up the world.

The description surely covers many of the salient features of the multinational phenomenon. The trouble is that it was written (with a few emendations by myself) by Lenin in 1917. This suggests that the phenomenon is not as new as we tend to think—or rather, that whatever is "new" about it cannot be discovered in the mere presence of great sums of capital invested by the enterprises of one country in the territory of another country.

Add to that the following disconcerting fact. According to the calculations of Myra Wilkins,* the value of total U.S. foreign investment in 1970 amounted to about 8 percent of U.S. gross national product. In 1929, long before the great multinational "acceleration" took place, it was 7 percent. In 1914 it was also 7 percent. Thus despite their increase in sales, despite the geographic relocation of investment out of the agricultural and mining belts into the industrial markets of the world, despite a change in the type of investment, away from plantations into factories, the global magnitudes of foreign investment remain surprisingly constant.

Of course, one is tempted to say that the shift into "high-technology" industry has hugely increased the economic leverage of this foreign investment. Has it? One could also argue that in an era of impending constraints on growth and technology, and increasing importance of food and raw materials, this very shift has also reduced their potential for economic power.

Can one, in the midst of so much confusion, make some sense of the multinational presence? With much trepidation, I shall try.

*Myra Wilkins, *The Maturing of Multinational Corporations,* (Cambridge, Mass.: Harvard University Press, 1974), p. 375.

We must begin by recognizing that the fundamental process behind the rise of the multinational corporation is growth, the urge for expansion that is the daemon of capitalism itself. Why is growth so central, so insatiable? In part the answer must be sought in the accumulative drive of a business civilization, a civilization in which the self-esteem and self-valuation of businessmen are deeply intertwined with the sheer size of the wealth they own or control.

But growth is also a defensive reaction. Companies seek to grow in order to preserve their place in the sun, to prevent competitors from crowding them out. Hence the struggle for market shares has always been a central aspect of the capitalist system, lending color to the robber baron age, taking on a more restrained but no less intense form in the age of the modern "socially responsible" firm.

A number of economists have described the dynamics of the typical stages of business expansion, from the small owner-operated factory to the managerially directed, multiproduct, multiplant "big business." Only recently, however, have we begun to describe the sequence of events that drives a firm to make the decisive leap across national boundaries, with all the headaches and problems that such a venture entails—foreign governments to deal with, foreign languages to speak, foreign currencies to worry about. Any number of stimuli may finally tempt an expanding company to make the leap. It may have begun to penetrate a foreign market with exports, and then may decide to locate a production facility abroad in order to avoid a tariff that impedes its exports. It may locate a manufacturing branch abroad to forestall—or to match—a similar step by one of its rivals. It may seek the advantages of manufacturing abroad because wages are cheaper —Hong Kong is the great example of this. One important explanation of the recent surge of multinationalization is the development of technologies of travel and information that make it possible for executives to visit distant plants, or to communicate with overseas subordinates, with little more trouble than with underlings on one U.S. coast or another.

This phenomenon of expansion, with its aggressive and defensive roots, emphasizes an extremely important aspect of what we call "multinationalization," which is that all the multinational companies are in fact *national* companies that have extended their operations abroad. They are not, as their spokesmen sometimes claim, companies that have lost their nationality. Two giant companies—Shell and Unilever—have in fact mixed nationalities on their boards of directors, and IBM never wearies of boasting that Jacques Maisonrouge, President of the IBM World Trade Corporation, is French. But I can see little evidence that IBM is not an "American" company, notwithstanding; and no evidence that any other of the giant multinationals cannot be unambiguously identified as having a distinct nationality. In fact, a study conducted in 1966 of the composition of 1,851 top managers of U.S. multinational corporations found only 1.6 percent to be of foreign nationality.*

* Kenneth Simmonds, in Courtney Brown, ed., *op. cit.*

This puts into considerable doubt a thesis that runs through much of the literature on the multinationals. When Richard Barnet and Ronald Müller write in *Global Reach* about the multinationals as the great colonizers of the future, they swallow whole the declarations of a few companies that they have risen above the parochial views of mere nationalism. Yet even Barnet and Müller speak of the advent of true multinationals, responsible to no one but themselves, as a possibility rather than an actuality. So, too, although Myra Wilkins' historic review of multinationalism sketches out a sequence of multinational organizations evolving from a "monocentric" to a "polycentric" form, in which the planets disengage themselves from the parent sun and wander about the economic universe on their own, she is hard-pressed to cite a case of the latter. (She suggests that ITT could properly have been called such a "true" multinational as early as the 1920s or 1930s, but recent events in Chile make one wonder how much ITT today is "above" the considerations of national identity.)

Thus I think we must view the world of very large, expansive national enterprises, extending their operations abroad, as a change in degree, not kind, from the world of very large expansive enterprises still contained within national borders. In a word, I think skepticism is in order when we ask whether the multinationals signal a radically new development in world capitalism.

Here it is useful to view the basic characteristics of present-day monopoly capitalism. An economy dominated by the kinds of expansive organizations I have described sooner or later encounters extreme difficulties of economic coordination. We do not know if a world of atomistic enterprises would run as smoothly as the theory of pure competition suggests, and we never shall know. We do know that an economy dominated by giant firms encounters serious problems in dovetailing its private operations so as to provide substantially full employment, maintain a stable level of prices, and produce the full array of goods and services needed by the population. As we have seen, in every capitalist nation this has led to what is euphemistically called a "mixed" economy—an economy in which the world of business is restrained, guided, subsidized, protected, buttressed by a growing array of public instruments and agencies. To repeat our central theme once more, governments, for all their ideological skirmishes with business, have always been the silent partners of business; indeed, as Adam Smith was explicit in declaring, private property would not exist a "single night" without government.*

Does the multinational change this basic picture? I do not think so in any fundamental way. I have already mentioned the erosion of "sovereignty" caused by the ability of the multinationals to locate their plants in this country or that one, or to transfer their profits from one nation to another by means of arbitrary pricing. But is this significantly different from the failure of nation-states to exercise control over companies—domestic or foreign—*within* their national boundaries? What effec-

*Adam Smith, *The Wealth of Nations*, (New York: Modern Library, 1937), p. 670.

tiveness does the United States have, for example, in directing the location of the investment of General Motors inside the United States, or for that matter in affecting the design of its products, its growth policies, etc.? What difference does it make to our national sovereignty if Valium or chocolate bars are made by a Swiss rather than a U.S. firm?

Of course, there are some differences, mainly having to do with the flows of funds across our national borders. But in the absence of the flows generated by the multinationals—the export of capital out of the United States, the import of profits back—there would be still the flows of funds generated by normal exports and imports, equally capable of working international monetary mischief, equally difficult to control.

The situation is somewhat different with regard to the underdeveloped countries. Foreign corporations play a powerful and sometimes pernicious role in determining the pace and pattern of the economic advance of these nations. They often support technologies and social structures that are inimical to the rounded development of the backward areas—for example, shoring up corrupt and privileged classes or encouraging countries to concentrate agricultural production on exports rather than on badly needed food for local consumption. The profits they earn in the underdeveloped areas are often extremely high.

But is this a *new* state of affairs? The company towns and plantation enclaves of an earlier era were in every way as deforming (and as profitable) as the operations of the multinationals today. It was, after all, under the drive of foreign capital that such countries as Brazil and Honduras and Rhodesia first became adjuncts of the modern industrial system, each producing a single commodity for a world market. If there is any remarkable change to be noted, it seems to be the long-overdue assertion of political independence on the part of these one-time economic colonies, and their attempts to impose much stricter forms of supervision over the dangerous foreign bodies embedded in their midst. Indeed, where is the process of the subordination of private international economic power to local political control more evident than in the places where the multinationals are most visible—the oil-producing regions of the world?

In suggesting that the role of the multinationals may be exaggerated, I do not wave away the change that these companies exercise vast influence, both overt and covert. I only maintain that this is an ancient condition. That the multinations represent a wholly new phase of capitalism is therefore a proposition of which I have become increasingly doubtful. The internationalization of production undoubtedly leads to new problems, both for the economic production mechanism and the political control apparatus of capitalism. But that is a very different thing from asserting that the multinationals have transformed capitalism in such a way as to reduce its political-economic tension, much less to resolve it in favor of the hegemony of the internationalized company.

Indeed, to my mind the rise to prominence of the multinational allows us to see more clearly than before the essential nature of this tension between business and the state. What we are witnessing at the moment, and are destined to see ever more clearly as we proceed into the future, is a conflict between two modes of organizing economic affairs—a "vertical" mode that finds its ultimate expression in the centrally organized, pannationally rooted structures of production, and a "horizontal" mode expressed in the jealously guarded boundaries of the nation-state. These same conflicting modes will persist if the multinational corporations become nationalized or converted into the economic arms of a centralized planned society, call it capitalism or socialism.

In this situation of conflict, it is entirely possible that both the power of the economic units and that of the state control system will be enhanced in the coming decades, the corporation-ministry embracing larger numbers of individuals—non-national as well as national—within its hierarchical framework, the state enforcing new limits of maneuver and prerogative on the economic entities within and beyond its borders.

But it seems impossible that in this contest between two modes of large-scale organization, that of economics will take ultimate precedence over that of politics. Men will go to great lengths to make money or to achieve economic status, and will submit to numbing routines to find their places in the productive framework of society. But even at its most successful, the corporation does not have the quasi-religious appeal of "identity" offered by the national state. Nor does the corporation have the capability of balancing, however crudely, the requirements of national survival against those of its own expansion. The political arm of capitalism will not therefore wither before the new tests posed by the multinational. Instead, it will eventually be strengthened and enlarged, reaching out in ways that were not necessary when the power of the corporation was roughly coterminous with that of the nation-state rather than extending into the areas of other nation-states. Multinational capitalism, in other words, although characterized by firms that extend their private operations to global dimensions, will be even more pressed in the direction of planning and political control than if the multinationals, by some miracle, vanished from the scene.

This is not an encouraging outlook for those who favor the extensive decentralization or dismantling of economic and political power. I share their wish to dissolve the massed power that is so much a force for human deformation in our times. I am fully in accord with the view that both corporations and nation-states are crude instrumentalities with which to deal with humankind en masse or as individuals. I would be the first to admit that governments, no matter how "postindustrial" or how "socialist," still depend on the organizing force of patriotism which remains the last refuge of scoundrels; and corporations, no matter how "multinational," are still propelled by motives better looked on askance than glorified and encouraged. As between the two, it is difficult to know which form is better suited—or less ill-suited—for the elevation of mankind.

97

Yet, in the face of the challenges that beset us today and loom in the future—challenges we shall examine in more detail in the last chapter—there seems to be no alternative to the extension of organization, control, and economic and political discipline over the activities of mankind. It is our hope that this extension of authority may in time wane, as the need for it lessens. From the study of other societies, mainly "primitive" cultures, we know that people can order their lives without the massive organizations we call "corporations" or "ministries of production" or "nation-states," by building them around the great supportive pillars of tradition or religious life. What we have not learned is how to introduce these modes of social organization into civilizations dedicated to the accumulation of wealth, or perhaps no less important, to the accumulation of scientific knowledge. In the period of the middle future, I suspect we shall have to utilize both the crude agencies of nationalism with its irrationality and force, and corporations or ministries with their hierarchies of status and inculcated dissatisfaction. A radical change in social organization that could rid us of these central mechanisms must await the transformation of society under the dissolving forces of the long run, a period that we can only dimly envisage. But that takes us to the consideration of what those dissolving forces may be, and of their implications for capitalism in the last phase of its existence.

FIVE

The Long Run

THIS FINAL CHAPTER brings us at last to a consideration of the question that has hovered in the background of our previous discussions. We must now address ourselves directly to the long-run challenges that beset capitalism, and that will, I believe, spell its demise.

Here the crucial problem is the meaning we assign to the words "long run." Few would deny, I am sure, that capitalism will eventually disappear. No civilization, save only the most primitive, lasts "forever," although some primitive civilizations—one thinks of the societies of New Guinea or of aboriginal Australia or parts of Africa—have shown astonishing staying power. But this is because they are static, changeless. A civilization built on the direct search for change, of which capitalism is perhaps the foremost example, can hardly be expected to enjoy an indefinite life span. Not even the staunchest defender of capitalism, I dare say, would assert that our business civilization will weather the next thousand years, or even the next five hundred.

But it is one thing to acquiesce in the eventual disappearance of a civilization, and another to expect its death within a more or less clearly defined period of time. Unless we do so, however, our speculations become little more than vague prophecies, robbed of

meaning because of their boundlessness. I shall therefore begin by venturing an estimate of the period I call
the "long run"—that is, the period beyond which
capitalism as a recognizable form of social organizations will cease to exist. I suggest that this long-run
termination of capitalism will occur within a century
—that is, within the lifetimes of our grandchildren or
great-grandchildren, barring, of course, a nuclear holo-
caust that would spell the extinction of all industrial
societies in their present forms.

Two reasons seem to me to define the life span of
our present system, or of its politicized successor. The
first of these is one to which we have now alluded many
times—the fact that we are leaving a historic epoch in
which the expansive drive of capitalism could be ac-
commodated by an indefinitely rich and vast environment and entering an epoch in which that drive must be
blunted and ultimately stopped by the progressively
intractable obstacles of nature.

Let me present this situation with all possible brev-
ity. Basically, the challenge arises because industrial
growth, or capitalist expansion, is an *exponential*
process—a process that procedes like a snowball, re-
quiring continuously increasing quantities of resources
and spewing forth continuously increasing quantities of
wastes, simply to maintain a constant pace of expansion. No social processes of an exponential character
are capable of indefinite continuance. Sooner or later all
such processes must overload their environment, consuming all its nutrients or poisoning it by the waste

products associated with growth. That is why curves that originally shoot upward in near-vertical fashion sooner or later bend into "S" shapes, or actually reverse themselves and go into decline.

The critical question is to determine where one is on a curve of growth—at some point where continued expansion may be possible for an extended period, or near the point of exhaustion of nutrients or the spoiling of the environment which must bring expansion to a halt or reverse it. Here is where the debate over resources and environment requires that we make some empirical estimates, however imprecise, as to our present position.

A good place to begin is with coal, the fossil energy resource available in the greatest quantity. It is estimated that the "ultimately recoverable" amounts of coal, which includes all of this resource thought to be located within the top kilometer of the earth's crust, would suffice to maintain our current rate of coal use for over 5,000 years. However, if our use of coal continues to expand at a rate of just over 4 percent a year—a conservative estimate, given the impending exhaustion of petroleum supplies—this same "ultimately recoverable" resource would be consumed within 135 years. The same exponential shortening of time spans applies to other materials, such as aluminum. It has been estimated that the top kilometer of planetary crust contains enough aluminum to last for 68,000 years at present rates of use. However, the present rate of *expansion* of use—about 6.4 percent a year—will exhaust this immense supply in a mere 140 years. Perhaps even more impressive is the application of exponential estimates to supplies of all minerals. Today we extract and use about 2.7 billion tons of the ten leading minerals each year. If our rate of use were to grow at a modest 3 percent a year for a thousand years, this would entail a weight of materials greater than that of the earth itself. In fact, it is doubtful that we could sustain our growth of these ten leading minerals for a period of 200 years.*

` Thus the exponential growth process that has been a central attribute of capitalism obviously cannot continue forever. Moreover, the period during which we can expect to fuel this process is much shorter than we might imagine. To be sure, the timetable for this impending resource exhaustion cannot be exactly specified because it depends on many imponderables: the invention of new extractive technologies, the development of synthetic chemistry, the discovery of means of disposing of vast mountains of tailings and wastes, the extension of capabilities for recycling materials. But the general considerations above are sufficiently impressive to give some credence to a time frame of a century as the maximum period during which we can expect our resource base to support growth at anything resembling current rates. Moreover these estimates do not take into account the likelihood that rates of resource use will rise, for a time, as the underdeveloped world attempts to bring its per capita utilization of the earth's minerals or energy to a par with the level of consumption in the advanced areas of the globe.

*These figures are based on calculations by Emile Benoit in a paper entitled "Must Growth Stop?," to be published in a collection of essays for Kenneth Boulding.

A second reason for anticipating a fixed life span for capitalism hinges on the problem of pollution. There are numerous "poisonous" effects associated with the industrial processes of capitalism, some of which enable us to establish rough orders of magnitude for the length of time during which continued growth will be compatible with social viability. Of these, perhaps the most formidable is that of inadvertent climate modification. Continued energy growth at existing rates of between 3 and 4 percent a year would generate major changes in local temperatures. In the opinion of Stephen Schneider, Deputy Head of the National Center for Atmospheric Research, this will "cause climate changes that could be both global and irreversible" after the year 2000.* Equally ominous is the threat of overheating the global atmosphere as a consequence of steadily adding manmade heat to the solar energy received by the sun. At present energy growth rates, in 150 years man-made heat throw-off will equal about 1 percent of the energy received from the sun. A continuation of these rates for another century would render the planet uninhabitable.

Here, too, of course, the specification of exact timetables is obscured by imponderables of technology and social organization. A changeover to energy sources that employ winds and tides and solar radiation would considerably delay the advent of a disastrous rise in atmospheric heat, although they would not affect the dangers of local climate modification. From the pollu-

*Stephen Schneider and Roger Dennett, "Climatic Barriers to Long Term Energy Growth," *Ambio,* 1975 (Boulder, Colo.: National Center for Atmospheric Research).

tion side, then, as well as from that of resource availability, we have some general empirical findings that make an estimate of 100 years a plausible approximation of the time span within which growth must come to a halt.

These containments of the future must bear on every form of civilization, save only those few pockets of self-sufficient, subsistence culture that may persist into the twenty-first century. Industrial socialist as well as industrial capitalist countries must yield before, and adapt to, the environmental constraints of a planet that is being rapidly pushed to the limits of its usable capacity. Hence, many of the difficulties to be faced by a business civilization will also impinge on other forms of economic society. Of these, the most important by far is apt to be the growing tension between poor nations and rich ones, whatever their social structures. This growth in tension could be averted by a redistribution of wealth on a vast scale, but such an effort surpasses realistic estimates of the altruistic impulse of the richer nations (and might surpass the technical problems of the transference of wealth, even if such an impulse existed). The tension might also be alleviated if we could arrange by international agreement for the poorer nations to have the lion's share of the world's remaining mineral and energy supplies, but that too seems to fly in the face of reasonable expectations of national behavior. And of course the tension might also be diminished if we could look forward to the emergence of a world government capable of claiming the allegiance of African tribesmen, Indian peasants, Chinese communards, and

American and Russian middle classes; but even to spell out the requisites for such a world government is to reveal the improbability of attaining it.

Thus the antagonism between the developed and the underdeveloped nations of the world seems certain to increase. Moreover, the antagonism is given a special importance because the means of nuclear destruction, already fairly widely dispersed among the world's nations, will be available to all but the poorest nations within a matter of a decade or two. The stage is thus set for an intensification of international rivalry, as the poor nations seek in vain to gain economic parity with the rich ones, while possessing something that resembles parity in their ability to inflict hideous and perhaps irreparable military wounds.

But these dangers, which hold terrible threats for "wars of redistribution," are not specifically dangers to the business civilization. Rich socialist nations are as exposed to these tensions as rich capitalist ones. The demise of capitalism, in other words, does not hinge on its nuclear obliteration. It seems certain to occur even if, as all mankind must hope, international conflict is held to a manageable level.

What are the reasons for expecting its demise? I discern three, all associated with the internal effects of the cessation of growth within the long run of a century. The first internal effect is the constriction of the expansive drive that has been the specific characteristic of the business system, evidenced in our own day by the bursting of corporate production beyond its national territory. The increasingly severe constraints on industrial growth must bring to a halt the consuming passion of a business civilization for private expansion.

In itself, this exhaustion of the "spirit" of capitalism will spell a profound change in the values, the ambitions, the morale of a business system, of which we shall speak more later. More important, however, is that the end of corporate growth will bring about the progressive elimination of the profits that have been both the means and the end of the accumulation of private property. A business society, confined within the straitjacket of a more or less fixed volume of output, must expect a steady erosion of profits, as economists from Adam Smith to Marx and Keynes have long recognized. Corporations forced to operate in a fixed economic space will soon compete away each other's profits, or will suffer a fatal squeeze between the pressures of wage earners for larger shares of revenues and the inability to increase revenues by expanding output.

In the middle run, this squeeze on profits can perhaps be alleviated by shifting corporate activity into "service" industries, or by a continuing penetration of foreign markets. In the long run, however, the constraints on industrial production must exert an immense pressure against the profitability of corporate activity; and the possibilities for continued multinational expansion, in a world of scarcities, bitter hostilities, and intensified desires for national self-sufficiency, seem very unlikely to last more than another few decades.

The unavoidable curtailment of growth thus threatens the viability of capitalism by removing the primary source of the profits that have been the sustenance of a business system. But suppose that profits are removed? Suppose that capitalism becomes, by degrees, a highly planned bureaucratic state in which corporations more and more resemble socialist trusts —according considerable privileges to their upper echelons, but no longer dependent on profits for survival?

Such a trustified, profitless, bureaucratic "capitalism" is certainly not unimaginable. But in the cessation of growth there still resides a serious—indeed, I think fatal—threat to the continuance of a business civilization. This threat lies in the removal of the safety valve by which the deep tension between the claims of labor and property has been lessened in the past.

Here we revert to our original discussion of capitalism as a system of privilege. For, however buried under ideology, there exists an inherent antagonism within a system where income is distributed by two entirely different principles—energy, intelligence, skill, and luck on the one hand, the brute claims of ownership on the other. This antagonism must be intensified when it becomes impossible to satisfy the claims of the working majority by granting it ever-larger absolute amounts of real income. The constraints on growth thus exert their most severe effect on the distribution of income. When output ceases to grow, the claims of the poor cannot be appeased by increments of income that do not come out of the pockets of the rich but out of larger total output. In a growthless economic system, the contest over incomes becomes a conflict over rights, and in this impending struggle I find it difficult to believe that the rights of property will not be ever more deeply invaded or ignored.

A second source of internal dissolution of the business system is allied with the first. It is the expansion of the planning apparatus whose roots and evolutionary course we have traced in previous chapters. As I have said before, planning is the inevitable next stage of capitalism, a stage that will assuredly attempt for a long time to preserve rather than destroy the structure of privilege central to a business civilization. But the inescapable rise of planning must also greatly strengthen the power of that congeries of technicians, scientists, and planners whose rise we have discussed as an aspect of the middle range of the future. The plannification of capitalism, in other words, however necessary for its survival in the middle run, is also a source of its extinction in the long run. For a hundred years hence, when the impact of environmental dangers is no longer a matter for speculation but for immediate alarm and control, planning requirements must far exceed anything that is compatible with either the prerogatives of property or the machinery of the market. In the face of extreme distributional tensions on the one hand and potentially lethal consequences of private economic activity on the other, the extention of public authority must reach into and displace private decision making, not only in the determination of incomes but in the choice and means of output.

Indeed, to the extent that the threats of the environment eventually force a dismantling of large-scale industrial processes, whether by foresighted planning or simply through localized disasters, political power is certain to be wielded without regard for any traditional criteria of a business system. Whether, in the long run, political authority will utilize "scientific" means of allocating resources and distributing incomes, or will simply impose a direct military discipline, we cannot foresee. But surely the claims of rents and interest and profits, the play of the market, or the right to conduct "private" enterprise will appear as archaic as the claims of royalty or nobility in the face of a democratic revolution.

These drastically changed aspects of the internal setting of capitalism—the end of business expansion and the extension of planning into every corner of economic life—offer two primary challenges to the continuation of capitalism, once the constraints of the long run begin to bear heavily on its operations. But they are attended by a third change that offers a threat of equal magnitude. This is the prospective erosion of the "spirit" of capitalism to which we have already referred.

Here we necessarily move even further into the realm of imponderables, and the possibility of ascribing a given time span disappears. Yet I do not think we should disregard the prospective decay of the value system of a business civilization because it is impossible to make hard and fast pronouncements with regard to the rate of its metastasis. So skeptical a social observer as Schumpeter was prepared, in the end, to pin his prediction of an end to capitalism on the change in its attitudes and outlooks. I suggest that we should also give due weight to the decay of business civilization from changes in its value structure.

Primary among these value changes I would place a waning belief in the ability of a business civilization to provide social morale. Traditionally, this morale has been pictured as arising spontaneously from the acknowledged capability of a business system to enhance the material well-being of its members. Few defenders of capitalism have tried to justify the system in terms of the nobility of its motivations or the spirituality of its aims. The defense of capitalism has always rested on the social contentment that was presumed to result from the release of mankind from its historic condition of material insufficiency.

This defense is already in doubt. For surely the business system has lived up to or exceeded the fondest hopes of its protagonists with respect to its productive virtuosity. What prodigies of material achievement the contemporary American enjoys as he drives over plains where his forebears trekked! What miracles of engineering does he not command to wash his clothes and his dishes, clean his teeth, shine his shoes, tell the time to the nearest tenth of a second, detract his incipient cancers, converse with friends in distant cities! Is he not only healthier and longer-lived than his forefathers, but better informed, better entertained—in a word, "better off" in nearly every measurable dimension?

But does not this recital reveal what has not been

gained as well as what has been gained? Is the contemporary American a better as well as a richer citizen than his antecedents? Is he more at peace with his children, his parents, himself? Is he wiser as well as more informed; happier as well as more pampered; sturdier and more self-reliant as well as better fed, housed, clothed, transported? To ask these questions, rhetorical though they be, is, I think, to express a hollowness at the center of a business civilization—a hollowness from which the pursuit of material goods diverts our attention for a time, but that in the end insistently asserts itself.

What is the nature of this hollowness? I would trace it primarily to two aspects of the business civilization that undermine the gains that material advancement undoubtedly confer. The first is the tendency of a business civilization to substitute impersonal pecuniary values for personal nonpecuniary ones. Consider, for example, the conversion of sport—one of the oldest and most stirring rituals of mankind—into a commercial enterprise, in which athletes are no longer heroes but money makers, games no longer contests for glory but for cash, and the mercenary qualities of participants, which would have been a source of shame in a Greek or medieval festival, are trumpeted aloud as an admirable character trait.

Or consider advertising, perhaps the single most value-destroying activity of a business civilization. Schumpeter spoke of the cold rationality that was to prove the undoing of the system. He ignored the extraordinary subversive influence of the relentless effort to persuade people to change their lifeways, not out of any knowledge of, or deeply held convictions about the "good life," but merely to sell whatever article or service is being pandered. I do not think we pay sufficient heed to the power of advertising in making cynics of us all: at a business forum I was once brash enough to say that I thought the main cultural effect of television advertising was to teach children that grown-ups told lies for money. How strong, deep, or sustaining can be the values generated by a civilization that generates a ceaseless flow of half-truths and careful deceptions, in which it is common knowledge that only a fool is taken in by the charades and messages that supposedly tell us "the facts"?

Moreover, there is, I think, a second reason why the material achievements of a business civilization fail to generate the satisfactions we expect of it. This is the disregard of business for the value of work. A business civilization regards work as a means to an end, not as an end to itself. The end is profit, income, consumption, economic growth, or whatever; but the act of labor itself is regarded as nothing more than an unfortunate necessity to which we must submit to obtain this end.

Now, of course, labor *is* a necessity on which material survival depends. In an environment of scarcity, even under the most enlightened and democratic government, work must be performed, some of which can be justified only in terms of the end to which it is directed. But the business civilization carries the disregard of work far beyond what is required by the objective necessities of survival even at a fairly high level of material enjoyment. Perhaps this is ultimately a fault that capitalism shares with industrial socialism—a fault whose roots lie in the machine process and the worship of efficiency. But this subordination of the act of labor to the overriding calculus of technology and efficiency is given a special blessing under a business civilization, where the values of output are celebrated and those of input merely calculated.

Here, too, along with the mindless commercialization of life, lies the basis for that vitiation of the spirit that is sapping business civilization from within. The way of life encouraged by the business process has proved disappointing not only with regard to its rewards but also with respect to its requirements. Thus at the very time that the mechanism of the business system must prepare to undergo an unprecedented trial, the participants in the system cannot be expected to rally to its defense with the enthusiasm of their parents or grandparents. Patriotism—or better, nationalism—may well be on the rise in our day, but economic patriotism is on the decline, especially for believers in the orthodox capitalist faith.

These considerations apply with particular force to the market mechanism that, along with private property, constitutes an essential characteristic of capitalism. The market in conventional theory is the means by which capitalism allocates its productive efforts and distributes its rewards without recourse to the alternative methods of tradition or command. It is vaunted, in the conventional textbooks, for its flexibility, its "efficiency," its capacity for matching social desire with social effort.

But the market mechanism also contains profound weaknesses that have been overlooked during the period of uninhibited capitalist expansion. One of these is its tendency to create extremely skewed distributions of income and property, a tendency that a straitjacketed economy will no longer accept with the forebearance of an expanding one. Another weakness is the failure of the market to protect us against the socially deleterious side effects of production, such as pollution, an aspect that becomes intolerable in a threatened environment. And a third weakness is the matter to which we have just referred—the exclusive focus of the market on economic activity conceived and measured in quantities of material output, not in qualities of human input. The market celebrates private consumption and ignores private production. This indifference to the experience of work corrodes and corrupts much of the way of life in a business civilization.

These "civilizational" challenges of the long run are also intimately associated with the prospect of a decline in, and finally a halt to growth. The cessation of growth removes the possibility of a ceaseless revindication of the business spirit through its self-justification in material aggrandizement. The values of acquisitiveness ill accord with the imperatives of material conservation. The sanctity of property will have to endure inescapable encroachments in the name of social survival. The prevailing system of business values must contend with technical or statist attitudes that will bring the commercial orientation of capitalism into disrespect or disregard. Is it possible to imagine the world a century hence, seeking to avoid material breakdown, bending every element of its political power to the curbing and redirection of the economic process, still open to the siren songs of an advertising mentality?

I suspect, then, that the cessation of growth will finally and fatally undermine a spirit that is already on the wane. On the one hand, the driving force of capitalist entrepreneurs will have been replaced by the carefully supervised calculations of state planners. On the other hand, the appetite for material growth will have been forcibly suppressed. Both the legitimacy and the functional purposes of private property and the market mechanism will have lost their claims for popular support. Perhaps most important of all, we can expect that this period of growing internal and external tension and heightened concern for survival is likely to produce its own values—nationalistic, religious—that will provide a needed new system of beliefs required to replace an outmoded one.

After capitalism, what? Not, I think, a "revolution." The demise of the business system is likely to proceed by degrees, insensibly altering a civilization that can be called "capitalist" into one that, whatever its appelation, no longer bears sufficient resemblance to the system we know to enable us to call it by the same name. We project the image of a tightly controlled society where the traditional pillars of capitalism—the legitimacy of private property and the operation of the market mechanism—have been amended beyond recognition, if not wholly superseded by state property and state directives.

Is such a postcapitalist system to be described as "fascism"? As "socialism"? I suspect that these traditional terms have little applicability to the political or economic structures of societies that, whatever their history, will be struggling to adapt to stringent and demanding environmental change.

Here I can do no better than to repeat a prognosis that I have expounded elsewhere.* It is to liken our distant prospects to those that followed the "'fall' of the Roman Empire—the century or so after the sack of Rome in which the established institutions of the Empire gradually lost their ability to cope with the orderly provision of the former Roman territories, and in which a deep and pervasive crisis of faith simultaneously destroyed the Empire from within.

The analogy leads me to the belief that, as in the case of the fall of Rome, the end of business civilization will not come about as a single dramatic event. Rome may have been sacked in 410 A.D., but a variety of semi-Roman political forms lingered on after that event: the Ostrogoth and Visigoth kingdoms, the colossus of Byzantium, the Carolingian "empire." In similar fashion, the decline of the business civilization may or may not be marked by some extraordinary event comparable

---

* See "Second Thoughts on the Human Prospect," in the third printing of *An Inquiry into the Human Prospect* (New York, W. W. Norton, 1975). This essay was originally presented at the Seminar on Technology and Social Values at Columbia University.

to the pillage of Rome, but it is also likely to be followed by a number of variant social orders, some of which may for a long time exhibit businesslike institutions or even some business-oriented values. Nonetheless, just as the fall of Rome eventually resulted in the disappearance of its central institutions and its "classical" spirit, so the successors to the civilization of business will sooner or later drift in a direction that will no longer bear much resemblance to the present order.

Here another Roman analogy may have significance for our long-term prospects. A crucial element in the transformation of the Roman system into the wholly different medieval period was the influence of the new religion of Christianity, which at first undermined the old order and later provided the spirit and shaped the institutional forms of the new order. So, too, in our future, I suspect that a major force for the transformation of business civilization will be a new religious orientation, directed against the canons and precepts of our time, and oriented toward a wholly different conception of the meaning of life and a mode of social organization congenial to the encouragement of that life.

What sort of religious orientation might this be? From our prior argument, a high degree of political authority will be inescapable in the period of extreme exigency we can expect a hundred years hence. This augurs for the cultivation of nationalist, authoritarian attitudes, perhaps today foreshadowed by the kind of religious politicism we find in China. The deification of the state, whatever we may think of it from the standpoint of our still-cherished individualist philosophies, seems therefore the most likely replacement for the deification of materialism that is the unacknowledged religion of our business culture.

This statist attitude, I should add, need not be one of a blind identification of secular rulers and divinity, comparable to the worst of the Roman emperors. Science and technology will be necessary partners with the state in defining the pace and pattern of economic life; and the "religion" of statism may therefore well include an admiration for scientific attitudes. What is crucial in the statist "religion," as I foresee it, is the elevation of the collective and communal destiny of man to the forefront of public consciousness, and the absolute subordination of private interests to public requirements. Whether this will be consistent with or conducive to political and intellectual liberties in general it is difficult to say. In principle, there is no reason why freedom of expression could not flourish in a survival-minded community. In practice, the centralization and intensification of political authority make this seem doubtful.

At a further remove, it is possible to imagine—one cannot "foresee"—an eventual dissolution of centralized power and a turn to the small-scale communities, based on self-sufficient and ecologically safe practices that have marked those enduring primitive worlds of which we spoke earlier. That is, perhaps, the destination toward which the constraints of nature are pushing the evolution of the social organism. But this achievement of communal society cannot possibly occur until the present unified structures of industrial production have been disassembled; until the threat of nuclear obliteration has been overcome once and for all; until the administration of economic life has been successfully internalized and no longer needs external sanction. All this is possible, but it is not on the agenda of the coming century, at least not for the industrial nations of the world.

I do not think that historians of the future will lament the disappearance of the business civilization. Who deplores the decline of Greek slavery, the end of the feudal relations between serf and lord, or the collapse of Mandarin China? Who will regret the passing of the conception of the "private" ownership of wealth that is patently social in origin and impact, or the end of the market mechanism with its efficiency in the attainment of every purpose save that of human development? The era of capitalism, once it is past, will be the occasion for amazement, perhaps even for a certain grudging respect, as Marx himself acknowledged in the *Communist Manifesto,* for it was capitalism, after all, that broke the bond of material servitude for humanity, even though it fastened upon it other social bonds that hobbled its potentialities in new ways.

Yet just as Periclean Greece or feudal Europe or imperial China were more than just economic forms of social organization, historians will surely see in capitalism more than its economic achievements and exactions. Here the balance sheet will be much more difficult to sum up. On the one hand, there is the crassness of outlook, the self-centeredness of behavior, so inextricably mixed with the idea of a business culture. This attitude is not, of course, peculiar to capitalism, although it may be peculiar to all commercial relationships. But it is in the nature of capitalist society that it has celebrated and made a norm of social values that are at least tolerated in other civilizations. No other civilization has permitted the calculus of selfishness so to dominate its lifeways, nor has any other civilization allowed this narrowest of all motivations to be elevated to the status of a near categorical imperative.

But it would be wrong to sum up business civilization solely in terms of the philistinism that is its ugliest aspect. Bourgeois culture has also brought into being, and permitted to survive, other aspects of the individualism that is implicit in its economic philosophy. The ideas of political equality and dissent, of intellectual adventure, of social nonconformity, however much hedged about or breeched in practice, owe much of their development to bourgeois thought. Thus there are assuredly glories to the civilization of capitalism as there were glories to slave Greece or feudal Europe or ancient China. The parliaments, the scientific explorations, the spirit of artistic innovation of the capitalist world are its acropoli, its cathedrals, its bronzes. The self-conscious intellectual, half within, half outside his bourgeois home, is perhaps its most important cultural figure. And of course the material creations of its business organizations are its inextinguishable mark. Much as we now inspect Chichén Itzá, the Great Wall, the pyramids,

Machu Picchu, so we may some day visit and marvel at the ruins of the great steel works at Sparrows Point, the atomic complex at Hanford, the computer centers at Houston.

Of all these attainments, that which is most difficult to appraise in terms of the future is the cultivation of the individualism that is so much a part of bourgeois economics, politics, thought, and art. Here is the crucial issue with which "socialism"—I use the word to describe whatever forms of society succeed the business civilization—will have to come to grips. Assuming away all the difficulties of bureaucracy, technology, or stubborn remnants of business habits, the great question to which an enlightened and humane "socialism" will have to address itself is the degree to which the individual will be encouraged to develop his or her unique attributes, differences, eccentricities.

This is not a question for which easy answers are available. For socialism will find its *raison d'être* in the deliberate cultivation of an "organic" society, one that establishes norms of behavior, shared moral standards, a unifying vision of its destination. But what will then be the bounds for the expression of private preferences? What will be the liberties accorded to artistic statements, social or sexual habits, political utterances?

No doubt the answers will depend to a large degree on the stringency of the constraints with which "socialism" will have to contend. But this is not the only problem. Much will also hinge on the conception of the nature of man himself—on his depiction as an infinitely malleable and plastic social creature, or as a being whose individualism ultimately reflects the uniqueness or the final autonomy of each person. The philosophy of individualism, which the capitalist epoch has nurtured and expressed, albeit in the grossest form, takes its strength from the assertion that there exists such a uniqueness, a final autonomy, within each individual. Like all deep beliefs, this is an untestable proposition. Whether it will survive the demands of the future I do not know. I only know that when I take the measure of capitalism, it is for me the element that, if it does not redeem the whole, at least offers the deepest reason to hope that not all of its civilization will disappear along with the business system.

Index

125

Index